101 CAREER TIPS:

PROPEL YOURSELF TO THE TOP!

by

Tony Vercillo

Editor: Marilyn Martin
Contributing Editor: James Holzer
Graphics: Andrews International
Typesetting and Layout: Fourth Dimension Graphix

ISBN 1-880530-01-5

Library of Congress Number:
91-76038

Printed in the United States of America

First edition

Published by:

Delta Sales
4195 Chino Hills Parkway
Suite 520
Chino Hills, CA 91709

(800) 393-9737
FAX (714) 393-9856

The key to success...
and...
the key to failure
is found in six little words...

WE
BECOME
WHAT
WE
THINK
ABOUT.

- Earl Nightingale

Dedication: I dedicate this work to my two children, Anthony Michael and Darien Alyxandra. The joy and laughter they add to my life makes all the difference.

Acknowledgements: I'd like to thank some very important people who provided encouragement and inspiration throughout my career. First, to my original mentor, John, for taking me off the streets of Brooklyn and teaching me "the ropes." To John T., a master at career management, who taught me about values and how to manage people. To my wife Kim, for supporting my career aspirations. Finally, to my mother, for all you have done for me.

TABLE OF CONTENTS

101 Career Tips: Propel Yourself to the Top!

"Expect to get to the top, and you will!"

Note: The recommendations made in this book do not constitute an endorsement. These self-help techniques are my personal preferences.

PREFACE

Are there true *secrets* of success? It depends on your definition of success. If success is a meaningful and exciting career, then success can be yours by following the tips outlined in this book.

The focus of ***101 Career Tips: Propel Yourself to the Top!*** is self-improvement. This book will also improve your chances for career success. It explains many proven techniques used by *"movers and shakers"* to scale the corporate ladder. I have personally used these tips to become a vice president of a $250 million corporation by the age of 32. These tips work!

Self-improvement is the key to the executive *washroom*, and a sure-fire way to avoid ending up in the *mailroom*. Self-improvement is a lifelong process of education. Your education must be viewed as a lifetime course in **adaptation**. Personal adaptability ensures that you will not get "programmed into obsolescence" as the world rapidly changes around you.

101 Career Tips delves into the success traits most top executives have in common. ***101 Career Tips*** addresses the following areas:

- ❑ *Landing the perfect job.*
- ❑ *Creating a "dynamite" resume.*
- ❑ *Dressing for success.*
- ❑ *Improving your ability to communicate.*
- ❑ *Taking action and improving your decision-making.*
- ❑ *Developing character traits that lead to success.*
- ❑ *Proven approaches for improving your skills.*
- ❑ *Time management techniques.*
- ❑ *Special sections "For Women Only."*

Not every tip will work for everyone. You will notice that certain tips have a recommended frequency of use. Test the frequency and find out what works for you. Don't let one failure deter you from reaching your goals.

Regardless of your age, present job, career stage or long-term career aspirations, ***101 Career Tips*** will help you find ways to maximize your potential. You will learn how to overcome career obstacles that hinder success.

There may not be one overall secret to success. There are, however, *101 ways* to improve your chances. **GO FOR IT!**

INTRODUCTION

A wise observer once said, *"There is always a job at the bottom."* Ask yourself: is it a job I want, or a career?

If you choose *job,* you have short-term thinking, the kind that often proves to be disastrous. You are the "unhappy camper" who pitches a tent and lets fate dictate the terms and conditions of your stay.

If you say *career,* you possess the long term mind-set of a Master Builder; one who adapts his or her world to personal objectives, dreams, and aspirations. A Master Builder heeds the words of George Bernard Shaw, who stated, *"A reasonable man adapts himself to the world; an unreasonable man persists in adapting the world to himself. Therefore, all progress depends on the unreasonable man."*

With this statement in mind, it is easy to understand why you need to be a **career strategist**. A career strategist carefully maps out the progress of his or her profession based on past experiences. These experiences become the basis of their long-term career strategy. A properly executed career plan will help you accomplish your vocational mission in life; that is, the sum total of your career goals and aspirations.

Here are some cold, hard facts:

- ❑ If unemployed, it can take up to seven months to find a new job.

- ❑ For most advertised jobs, there are 300 - 350 applicants.

- ❑ Career counselors estimate there are more than 20,000,000 resumes in circulation on any given day!

- ❑ Reports estimate that millions of jobs will be eliminated in 1992 due to "downsizing" and "restructuring," which are buzzwords for layoffs and hiring cutbacks.

- ❑ You can expect 3 - 4 career changes and as many as seven different jobs during your lifetime. Unless you invest time and energy planning for these changes, your career transitions will be difficult and costly.

- ❑ The 1991 Northwestern Lindquist-Endicott Report of 259 American businesses stated that approximately 4% fewer college graduates were hired in 1991 than were hired in 1990. Estimates are the number will climb to 10% in 1992.

Intense competition is in store for career seekers in the turbulent 90s. According to Victor Lindquist, "*Not only are you competing with your classmates for fewer jobs, but also with those with experience already in the market looking for jobs.*" Those who did find jobs were paid an average of 2.7% higher in 1991 than they were paid in 1990, a figure hardly keeping pace with inflation.

101 Career Tips is a survival guide that takes into account "the slings and arrows of outrageous fortune" that stifle your progress. It is designed to aid college students, entry level and middle managers, and anyone else interested in furthering his or her career and maximizing income potential.

101 Career Tips will show you how to design a personalized success strategy to help steer clear of common, career-destroying pitfalls. Use the *101 Tips* outlined in this book, and you will *mastermind a personal plan* that will propel you to the top of any organization.

The book covers four major areas:

- ***Marketing Your Services.***
- ***Personal Organization.***
- ***Image and Perceptions.***
- ***Personal Edge Techniques.***

By investing in personal development, you not only increase your chances for success but also improve your self-esteem and general outlook on life.

Don't tackle all *101 Tips* at once. Take one step at a time, and remember...

SUCCESS IS JUST AN IDEA AWAY!

PART I. MARKETING YOUR SERVICES

Winning the career game takes planning. In the words of cosmetics queen Mary Kay Ash, "*Most people plan their vacations better than they plan their lives.*" A strong career plan will improve your chances for success. A career plan will also help you find your *passion* in life.

This section will help you get started and provides a framework for career planning. You will learn how to market yourself effectively by capitalizing on your key strengths and minimizing your weaknesses.

When Seeking Employment:

Tip #1: Twenty steps for getting the position you want.

❑ Target a career and position in your field that excites and interests you. It may be new territory for you, so make sure your skill-set matches the tasks expected of you.

❑ Target a geographic work location. This is a matter of personal preference. If you are single and mobile, you may have no problem relocating to another city, state or country. On the other hand, a married homeowner with children may not wish to relocate for family reasons or commute more than one hour a day each way.

For those willing to relocate, here's a list of ten "hot" cities *Money* magazine targeted as places to live and work in the 90's.

- Atlanta, GA
- San Diego, CA
- Boston, MA
- Chicago, IL
- Minneapolis/St. Paul, MN
- Dallas, TX
- Los Angeles, CA
- Washington, D.C.
- Phoenix, AZ
- Columbus, OH

- ❑ Analyze your potential. Ask yourself: What are my key strengths? The answer to this question is of utmost importance. It is a favorite of job interviewers.

- ❑ Invest in continued training and education. Education is a lifelong process. Our world is never ending arena of change demanding new skills and different approaches to problem solving. Technology is changing every day. For example, by the year 2000, experts forecast computers will be *50 times more powerful* than they are today.

- ❏ Outline a plan to zero in on the position you want. Learn what you can about the position before the interview. Learn the responsibilities and the pay scale. Prepare a budget that includes expenses for purchasing new clothes, travel, grooming and resume preparation.

- ❏ Prepare a personal biography and data sheet. This sheet should include everything there is to know about you. While some of this information is already on your resume, a detailed personal data sheet will get you in touch with ***who** you are* and ***what** you've done.* A one page personal biography written in a "How I've Spent My Life So Far" way can be a big help in clearing the cobwebs to help you focus on how to best realize your potential.

- ❏ Update your resume every four months (see ***Tip #6***). If four months pass and there is nothing new to add to your credentials, it's a sure sign you're not making progress.

- ❏ Apply for numerous positions. Don't be pigeonholed by a specialty. Apply for positions that not only directly fit your background and education, but also for positions where you can make use of your skills in another capacity.

- ❏ Obtain magic letters of recommendation. Carefully worded and highly personal letters from important people (past employers, community leaders, professors) go a long way in selling you to prospective employers. Be sure to include a phone number where your references can be reached. Encourage the interviewer to call them.

- Learn the language of the industry, *the lingo.* Get a copy of the company's annual report by calling their Public Relations department. Scan the report for performance measures the company deems important. Select jargon from the report so you can use it during the interview process.

Caution: Don't overdo it! It borders on the ridiculous to spout lines such as:

"I would handle the inquiry like any R.O. (repair order). If that fails, let's boot the dink (customer) back to the people in F & I (finance & insurance department)."

- Prepare job application forms. Complete these forms seriously and legibly. Don't appear to be annoyed when asked to fill out an application. Regardless of how comprehensive your resume, complete the application with a smile.

- Go on informational interviews (see ***Tip #18***). An informational interview can sometimes turn into a serious job prospect!

- Learn all you can about the firm. Go to the library and research as much information about the company as you can.

- Dress for success. You can't go wrong with dark conservative colors, shoes polished and appropriate accessories.

- ❑ Use time management. Be on time for your own party! Get to the interview five minutes early. Prior to the interview, spend time in the rest room giving yourself a pep talk, straightening your clothes, fixing your hair, and washing and drying your hands — no wet handshakes!

- ❑ Never underestimate the importance of getting to meetings early. Be polite, and make a good impression on the front office people. Decision makers often ask their administrative assistants or associates for their opinion about you. Being perceived as "one of us" versus one who does not fit into the corporate culture plays a big part in getting a position.

- ❑ Relax. Be natural. Be yourself. Don't be a phony or pretend to be something you're not.

- ❑ Sell yourself! Exude confidence and be proud of your accomplishments. It's not bragging if you can really do what you claim. Be enthusiastic and smile.

- ❑ Be perfectly frank about money. Know your worth in terms of salary, benefits and perks. Accept nothing less. If you come from weakness by making statements like "Whatever you offer is fine," or "I don't know. What is the position paying?" the interviewer will lose respect for you and attempt to hire you for less money.

  You may have received advice that "it's tricky to discuss money during an interview." Not true. Once you develop a rapport, the interviewer will usually ask the right questions:

  "What are you looking for in terms of salary? What do you want in terms of overall compensation?"

When you are prepared to answer these questions, it's a snap. You will have done your homework and know what the position pays; i.e., $28,000 a year, full dental and medical, company car and a three week vacation. Feel free to ask for more. If you do not speak up, you will never know if more was possible.

The art of negotiation demands a *Win!/Win!* outcome. It's in the interviewer's best interest to hire the most qualified candidate for less overall compensation. Saving money for the company is another feather in their cap.

What if there is no way for you to estimate the level of compensation? In this case, just ask:

"What is the salary range for this position?" Fixed salaries are rare; a salary range is usually established based on experience, accomplishments and reputation.

The interviewer replies: "Anywhere from $28,000 to $34,000 a year."

Immediately respond, "*$34,000 a year sounds right to me!*"

You have turned the tables on the interviewer. It will be very difficult for them to deny the salary that, in their own words, is "acceptable" to their organization. By keeping the salary on the high side, you leave room to negotiate and make everyone involved a winner.

❑ Watch for indications that the interview is over. If the interviewer is yawning and not paying attention, the interview is over. If the interviewer is sending signals through body language or making subtle negative remarks, help them end the interview.

BRING IN A RELIEF PITCHER

If you sense the interview is not going well, use the following tips to "save" the session:

1. Find a topic of common interest. Try to liven up the conversation by discussing a topic you know the interviewer enjoys. Discreetly look around the interviewer's office. Look at his or her bookshelf for books you may have read. Determine if the interviewer has received awards (any trophies?) you can ask about.

2. Analyze the situation. Maybe you are stressing the wrong skills. Try to change the focus of the discussion and emphasize the variety of your skills.

3. Ask the interviewer if you can go back to a question you believe you answered insufficiently. You might ask, "Is it okay if we go back to a previous question. I'd like to add to that discussion."

4. Be direct. Ask the interviewer if something is wrong. Find out if you said anything that may have been taken out of context.

- ❑ Write follow-up letters of appreciation to everyone you meet during your career campaign.

  Understanding these 20 Steps* will increase your chances of finding employment. They also provide a successful interview framework you can use throughout your career. For more information on these 20 steps, read *20/20 Career Planning* by Elizabeth Stockton available through Career Publishing (800) 854-4014.

* The twenty steps in ***Tip #1*** were adapted from *20/20 Career Planning* by Elizabeth Stockton.

SOME WORDS ABOUT WOMEN

Statistics show that women expect to receive less compensation than their male counterparts. American women are paid approximately 67% of what men make for doing the same work. By the year 2000, this figure will be over 80%, so hold your ground! Women can, and will, earn more money than they currently do. Women in Sweden, for example, already earn 91% of what men do.

Tip #2: Select a comprehensive public or college library and familiarize yourself with its many businss directories and reference volumes.

There are a number of directories that could help improve your career outlook. Here are a few found in the reference section of your library.

- ❑ *Standard and Poors Directory*
- ❑ *The Directory of Executive Recruiters*
- ❑ *Career Employment Opportunities*
- ❑ *Career Information Center*
- ❑ *Career Choice Encyclopedia*

These publications are worth their weight in gold when seeking employment.

Create your own reference library. Every year, libraries sell year-old copies of business directories for pennies on the dollar. These directories will prove to be valuable two to three years from initial publication.

Tip #3: Get hold of a glossary of industry terms.

Many large companies publish glossaries for entry level employees. Knowing the appropriate company jargon can improve your ability to communicate and will assist you in getting your message across during the interview phase.

The company annual report is a good source of inside information. You can request annual reports from a company's public relations department, or any large brokerage firm that is a transfer agent or trader of their stock.

Tip #4: Create the perfect resume.

Resumes **SHOULD:**

- ❑ Be one page long, or if absolutely necessary, one and one-half pages.
- ❑ Show progress in your education and career. Show not only where you've been, but where you are going.
- ❑ Be printed on ivory, light grey or white bond paper.
- ❑ Be businesslike and professional in tone.
- ❑ Reveal your leadership ability; i.e., public offices held, high-ranking military experience, community projects you initiated, participation in charitable organizations, and senior memberships in clubs, industry associations, fraternities or sororities.
- ❑ Mention only prestigious references. Nothing is more trite than resumes offering "References upon request." This implies "I have references, but they are not very important." If you knew President Bush on a first name basis, wouldn't you mention him as a reference? Get two noteworthy references with "marquee value" in your industry or community. List their names and business telephone numbers.

- ❑ Use the correct slant. If you are looking for a managerial position, structure the resume in chronological order starting with your present position followed by no more than three past positions. If you are marketing your skills, the resume should highlight your abilities; e.g., typing speed, word processing, number of software packages you know, etc.

VIVA LA VITA

One of the most important sections of your resume is the career objective outline. Don't make the mistake of using, "*A job in sales with a progressive company.*" Instead, call this section your ***Career Choice***. The implication is that you have made a conscious choice to follow a specific career path. The career choice section should read something like, "**Account Executive position in the Cosmetics Industry**."

Resumes **SHOULD NEVER:**

- ❑ Include age, weight or marital status.
- ❑ Reveal ancient history or "war stories."
- ❑ Display time gaps in your work history.
- ❑ Include political or religious affiliations.
- ❑ Include race or nationality.
- ❑ Include a photograph.
- ❑ Embellish your credentials.
- ❑ Criticize past employers, associates or professors.

A resume can be the difference between getting or losing an interview. Many initial interviews have been granted to individuals who invested time and resources in developing their resume.

Tip #5: Never underestimate the power of an informal, handwritten note.

GUTSY MOVE

Edward Bulwer-Lytton once said, "***The pen is mightier than the sword.***"

Regularly write thank you notes, congratulatory memos and sophisticated fan letters to authors, political candidates and CEOs. Note their accomplishments, but don't fawn over them as objects of worship. The object of this "*gutsy move?*" In return, you may receive letters that will bolster your credentials when job prospecting.

Caveat: *Be sincere — only write to those you genuinely admire.*

When Employed:

Tip #6: Update your resume every four months.

Be sure to include accomplishments not in your previous resume. Start each sentence describing your accomplishments with action verbs such as *supervised, delegated, improved, monitored, prepared, directed, initiated, controlled,* etc.

Keep your resume and credentials (recommendations, praise letters, awards, certifications) current. Updating your resume three times a year ensures key accomplishments get recorded and not forgotten. It also determines your degree of progress. Keeping your resume updated places you in an advantageous position should a hot career opportunity arise.

Your resume is a direct reflection of your professionalism. Have your resume prepared by an expert (they can be found in the Yellow Pages), or buy guides such as *15 Tips On Writing Resumes* by Freda Grones; *Just Resumes: 200 Powerful Resumes* by Kim Marino; or computer software such as Resume Writer or Perfect Resume.

It's not What you know, but Who you know!

Tip #7: *Network, Network, Network!*

Be a social extrovert (see ***Tip # 9***). Networking will help you establish new contacts. Where do you start?

The average person knows 250 people relatively well. Keep a follow-up system to ensure you stay in touch with friends, business associates and colleagues. They can be a good source of information, expertise and additional business contacts.

Attend community events such as Chamber of Commerce meetings, Breakfast Clubs and Cocktail Mixers. Don't neglect sports clubs, gyms or local sporting events. There are certain "executive" sports that attract the kind of people you want to meet: boating, horseback riding, tennis, golf, flying, rock climbing and jet skiing.

Networking involves staying in touch with people you meet. Although you won't strike gold at every networking meeting, your efforts will pay off in the long run.

One way to increase your business network is to collect business cards. When you meet someone, always ask for a business card. Keep it on file.

Tip #8: Join industry and networking organizations such as the *American Management Association*, *The Society of Automotive Engineers*, the *Jaycees* and the *Rotary Club* (ask your librarian for the latest listings for these and other organizations).

Industry-related associations provide a wealth of contacts, speaking forums and information on future management trends. Joining industry associations is also a good way to meet people who can make a difference in your career.

For example, I belong to the *World Future's Society* [(301) 656-8274] to stay on top of "things to come." They publish an excellent newsletter. It focuses on what futurists believe is a look at the next 100 years.

Tip #9: Stay in Touch.

To paraphrase Woody Allen, "*Success, for the most part, is just a matter of showing up.*" If people don't know how to contact you, how can they help you attain your goals?

Keep friends, colleagues and business associates informed of your whereabouts. Statistics show that some young professionals relocate an average of three times in a two year period! Stay connected. Send letters to everyone in your sphere of influence each time you move or change employers.

When you meet new and interesting people, send them a short letter expressing excitement in meeting them. Thank them for their time and suggest you stay in touch.

Style guides and sample letters will make your job easier. Books with examples of informal and business-like letters are in your local library or bookstore. Never copy these letters verbatim. People will recognize form letters and probably discard them.

Networking means more than just staying in touch with friends, business associates and colleagues. It is the best way to maintain your contact network and increase your people resource capabilities. Networking will be an invaluable tool throughout your career.

Make your networking count. Make it a point to know small, personal details about your contacts. Keep a file of particulars: birthday, anniversary, name of spouse, children, favorite hobbies and sports teams. Send them appropriate greetings or a clipping of a newspaper or magazine article of interest to them. The more you know, the better you can personalize your communications and "touch" them on an emotional level.

Tip #10: Attend company sponsored events to mingle with co-workers and converse with key executives in an informal setting.

Much of what is known as "underground business" takes place at company picnics, awards banquets and outside affairs.

Be sure to exude confidence, enthusiasm, cooperation and business savvy when dealing with upper management. Don't unduly monopolize a key player's time. Be a model team player: eager, friendly, helpful, creative and positive.

Golf is possibly the best way to bond with the kind of people who can benefit your career. If you can play golf well, you will be in big demand as a golfing partner. Many important deals are consummated on golf courses.

Tip #11: Call members of other departments during your first 90 days on the job.

Offer your assistance and comradeship with no strings attached. Suppress the tendency to be a self-proclaimed expert. Never be arrogant or condescending when offering advice and assistance. Be genuine and sincere in your approach, always concerned with team success. The ability to get along with others is an essential success trait.

Don't be the Anointed One! Be The Appointed One!

When you can genuinely add value, volunteer for company task forces, committees and focus groups. This will teach you how to be more effective in groups and establish your reputation as a "doer." *Integrity* is the keyword. Act with absolute integrity in all your dealings. In one survey, over 100 American CEOs rated ***integrity*** as the most important factor in the success of any executive.

Tip #12: Be an **Entrepreneur** within your department — an ***Intrapreneur!***

Initiate new projects, start a customer service revolution in your department, or espouse a cutting edge management approach; i.e., *Total Quality Management.* Employers appreciate those willing to take action and prudent risks.

Learn about *Process Value Analysis* which appears to be one of the hottest management approaches for the 90's. *PVA*, as it is called, deals with reducing the complexity of any process. When analyzing a given process, *PVA* asks the following three questions:

1. *Can the process be eliminated?*

2. *Can the process be simplified by reducing the non value-added tasks associated with the process?*

3. *Can the process be optimized by changing the design, the tasks, the number of required steps, etc.?*

I call this approach to Process Value Analysis, *ESO: The Three-Step Process Toward Continuous Improvement* (**ESO: E**liminate it, **S**implify it, **O**ptimize it). To learn more about Process Value Analysis, read the book, *Business Process Improvement*, by Jim Harrington.

Tip #13: Perform volunteer work in your community or begin a relationship with a charitable organization.

Offer services that complement your field of expertise. For example, if you are a gourmet cook, offer to serve meals to the needy during the holiday season.

From a public image standpoint, many corporations find it valuable to take strong positions with charities. They often assign "pet charity" duties to their best and brightest management executives. The opportunity to meet and mix with decision makers is always present.

Black tie charity events may be the only way for you to rub shoulders with the CEO of your company. For the price of a ticket and formal wear rental, you have a great chance of getting to know the boss in a safe, elegant setting. Attending a socially conscious affair will show you to be socially aware and concerned with your company's public image.

Be sure to put your heart into volunteer efforts. The old adage, "*give and you shall receive*" clearly applies.

Tip #14: Job enrichment makes sense.

Job enrichment, or *cross-training*, will give you a broader perspective on how your company works, and where you fit in the scheme of things. This is the age of the "*Totalist*" where hands-on knowledge of every aspect of your company will give you a "step up" on the executive ladder.

Request a lateral career move to market your services internally. Accepting a lateral move to another position or department will broaden your business perspective. The higher you go in an organization, the more well-rounded you must be.

Should you leave the organization, you will find your new skills valuable for making you a more marketable commodity.

BE A MARKETEER, NOT A MOUSE-KATEER!

To find out more about how to become an effective *marketeer*, read the book *Marketing your Services* by Dorothy Leeds. You can find this informative book at major bookstores. The book is divided into five parts:

- ❑ *How to Find the Job of Your Choice.*
- ❑ *Success Factors: The Ten Most Marketable Skills.*
- ❑ *Knowing your Product.*
- ❑ *Knowing your Market.*
- ❑ *Closing the Sale.*

Tip #15: Do not industry "hop" early in your career.

Prospective employers look for stability and a sense of purpose when reviewing resumes.

Industry Hopping is Far Different than Job Hopping

Let's say you take a managerial position at Coca Cola. Five years later Pepsi offers you double your salary. You move. Four years later, a major Midwestern soft drink distributor offers you a position as vice-president of marketing. You take it. To prospective employers and executive recruiters, you are a winner whose star is on the rise.

On the contrary, should you move from the beverage to the medical industry to the computer industry, you will seem like someone who doesn't have career direction. This is not an ironclad rule. If you happen to be a specialist in computer systems or accounting, industry choice is not as critical.

Remember, "*If you find **who** you are, you will get **what** you want!*"

Regardless of Your Employment Status:

Tip #16: Know yourself before attempting to sell your services.

Assess your key strengths and weaknesses. Compare your characteristics and traits to the following success profile. These traits have been found to be common in most effective top-level executives.

- ❑ *LEADERSHIP/IMPACT:* Do you possess charisma, a special personal presence felt by those around you? Do you feel good about your accomplishments? Do people feel you are honest and have integrity? Can you inspire people to follow you?

- ❑ *INTERPERSONAL SKILLS:* Do you make people feel at ease during conversations? Do most people genuinely like you? Are you a team player?

- ❑ *COMMUNICATIONS SKILLS:* Do you communicate in a direct and powerful manner? Can you write memos, letters and proposals that get response? Can you clearly articulate your thoughts in an organized fashion?

- ❑ *DECISIVENESS:* Do you have the ability to make quick, intelligent decisions? When necessary, can you muster an aggressive, assertive attitude?

- ❑ *ORGANIZATION/PLANNING SKILLS:* Do you plan activities in advance paying special attention to details? Do you possess consistent time management skills? Do you plan projects ahead of time so that you have thought them through before beginning them?

- ❑ *ADAPTABILITY/FLEXIBILITY:* Are you willing to change the status quo? Are you comfortable with change? Do you consider other points of view?

- ❑ *CREATIVITY:* Are you a creative problem solver? Do you generate a lot of ideas? Do you use both logical and intuitive thinking when making decisions?

Suggestion: Consider getting training in Creative Problem Solving. Call the *Center for Research in Applied Creativity* at (416) 648-4903.

- ❑ *STRESS TOLERANCE:* How do you react to stressful situations? Do you hang in there? Stay calm? Can you work effectively when under stress?

- ❑ *JUDGMENT:* Do you use sound judgment when making decisions? Do you make decisions without personal bias?

- ❑ *ANALYTICAL ABILITY:* Can you properly analyze problems and make good recommendations?

- ❑ *ENERGY/ENTHUSIASM:* Do you approach work with vigor and vitality — no hitting the snooze alarm two times each morning before getting out of bed? Are you driven to succeed? What kind of attitude do you possess? Positive? Enthusiastic? Self-Assured? Hard-Working?

- ❑ *PEOPLE MANAGEMENT SKILLS:* Do you truly know how to manage people? Do you balance your concern for results with a concern for people?

- ❑ *RESILIENCY:* Do you bounce back with strength and confidence after experiencing defeat? Do you regard setbacks as learning experiences, and savor them with the same level of energy you do your successes?

Solicit feedback regarding your strengths and development needs from supervisors, friends and loved ones. After determining your key strengths and weaknesses, map out a plan such as supplemental training or attending seminars to overcome your weaknesses.

Be patient, because behavior modification takes time.

Every 90 days, chart your progress and share the results with those best able to give you an unbiased critique.

One of the most important skills is leadership/impact. If you identified leadership skills as a weakness, I recommend you attend the *Dimensions in Leadership* seminar conducted by *The Center for Creative Leadership.* For a seminar date in your area, call: (919) 545-2810.

When selling your services, *sell* to your strengths and avoid tasks you've identified as weaknesses. For example, if you are not a good problem solver, stay away from tasks requiring analysis and evaluation until you have received the necessary training.

Tip #17: Plant enough seeds and something is bound to grow.

Every 120 days, answer targeted classified ads by sending your resume. This tactic is not necessarily a way to farm for a new job, but a means to gain added visibility. You can estimate your worth in the marketplace and make future contacts.

Today's job market is a rapidly fluctuating environment. Many employers keep resumes on file for years, calling candidates many months after they receive a resume.

Play it safe! Prospect only those classified ads with a specific company name. Avoid blind ads with no phone number and a P.O. Box address. These ads are often placed by executive recruiters to farm for candidates.

Sometimes these blind ads are placed by companies who do not want to alert an employee of plans to replace them. What if your company placed the blind ad and your resume ends up in the hands of your personnel manager?

Tip #18: Keep your interview skills sharp by going on one informational interview every year.

You can secure interview appointments by sending resumes to target companies on a regular basis. Another avenue to secure informational interviews is through *Job Fairs* or *Career Days*. You can find these events in the business and classified sections of your Sunday newspaper.

Going on interviews keeps you on your toes. Not only will you increase your business network, but you'll also be able to estimate your worth in the marketplace.

Remember, prospective employers look for professionals doing the jobs they want filled. Executive recruiters or "head hunters" get big commissions convincing prospects to switch companies for higher compensation. They live by the axiom, "It's easier to place a working candidate than an unemployed one."

Mail your resume to Executive Recruiters and Employment Agencies. Many Employment Agencies have recruiters on staff but don't advertise this specialty. They are listed in the *Yellow Pages* under Employment Agencies, Employment Temporary and Executive Search Consultants.

Another good source for executive recruiting firms is the library. Ask for the *Directory of Executive Recruiters*, a Kennedy publication.

Going on informational interviews is even more important in the 90s due to the uncertainty of the economic climate. Stories abound of executives who rebuffed an executive recruiter's offer, only to receive the dreaded *Pink Slip* two week later.

It's a numbers game. The more interviews you go on, the more likely you will land the position of your choice. Treat each interview as a learning experience. In time, your experience will pay off.

Keep informational interviews to yourself. Don't tell co-workers or take calls from an interviewer at work. If your motives and loyalty are questioned, explain your actions away as "*A fact-finding mission to stir my creative juices.*"

More on Investigating the Job Market

Roughly 75% of all jobs go unpublished. Finding the right job in the Sunday Classified Section can be a frustrating and intimidating affair. With this in mind, a question arises: if less than 25% of the jobs are advertised, is reading the want ads a waste of time?

Hardly. Read want ads daily. Some small companies advertise from Monday through Friday at a lower space rate to stand out from the Sunday ad jungle. Others want their ads seen on Sunday when the largest number of people are looking. Serious job hunters read ads daily. Some recruiters even give extra consideration to those who respond to midweek ads (everyone reads and responds to Sunday ads — be different, respond to midweek ads).

Look for leads and contacts. Read the want ads in a way that "searches" for the job market within the job market.

Tap the hidden job market of word of mouth and referrals by keeping your resume circulating.

In addition to answering obvious job "fits," send resumes for jobs in which you may be under-or-over qualified. Employers are sometimes unable to find the perfect candidate and may be willing to modify their requirements.

Don't hesitate to send resumes to companies you responded to earlier. Some companies have no means of tracking resumes. Your resume may get lost in a file or tossed in the trash for some reason. Follow up with a call and ask if your resume was received.

Never restrict yourself to categories. When seeking a Mechanical Engineering position, don't look just under "Mechanical Engineer." Positions are spread throughout the classifieds under different headings. Ads for Mechanical Engineers are sometimes listed under sub-headings such as Computers, Automotive, Aerospace, or Medical.

Don't neglect the Business section of the newspaper as a source for obtaining interviews. Carefully analyze company promotions, transfers, buy-outs, mergers and acquisitions. These company moves and shake-ups can open doors. Send an informal query letter and a resume to the key decision makers. If they like what they see and forward your resume to the personnel department, their blessing will carry a lot of weight.

In the end, your networking ability will be the deciding factor that sets you apart from the competition being considered for top spots.

Tip #19: Initiate ties and forge connections with a major university.

Offer to write for the university's newsletter. If you have credentials, offer to speak before undergraduate classes.

I was asked to speak before a graduate class at my alma mater, *United States International University.* I used the opportunity to test the topic, *Unleashing Your Creative Genius*, which became an audiocassette series. The school promoted the event with press releases and school notices.

A university can be a major source for up-to-date research and working papers in business, management and technology.

Tip #20: Get published!

The power of providing information will put you on the path toward building a special brand of credibility. You can begin by writing articles for school newsletters (your alma mater perhaps) and industry magazines. When you publish articles, you gain the status of an authority, an "expert," in your chosen field.

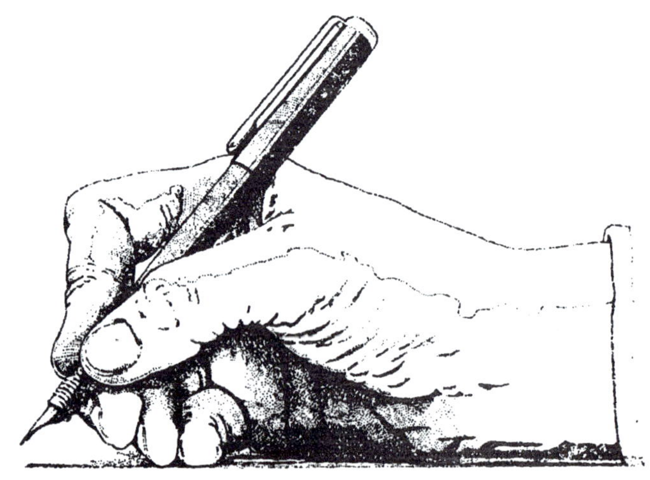

By publishing a small booklet entitled ***101 Fleet Tips***, I increased my reputation as an expert in the area of fleet and distribution management. This led to the publication of ***Passionate Leadership: Ten Powerful Principles That Will Change Your Life!*** Then came speaking engagements, and radio and television interviews.

My writing efforts continued and led to the book you now have in your hands. Two months following the completion of this book, I finished the script for the audiocassette series entitled, ***Unleashing Your Creative Genius***.

You may be saying to yourself, "Writing, sure. That's easy for you to say." True, some people are born with the talent to write. There is no reason, however, why you cannot master the basics of business writing.

Don't expect to join the editorial staff of *The New York Times* at first — this is pro territory. Writing articles for a school newspaper is a logical start, but even this can be tough competition. You will have to compete for space with writers who plan careers in journalism. Be persistent, and eventually you will find a topic that interests the editor.

Look to the many free, consumer-oriented regional publications distributed in your area. These publications often depend on freelancers for stories. Amateur writers looking to amass "clips" to show to larger publications can use these local magazines and newspapers to develop credentials.

Analyze these publications and see where you fit. Find the name of the publisher or editor. Send them a one page query letter telling them of your desire to write on a particular subject.

Here are some subjects for articles.

- ❑ *Restaurant Reviews*
- ❑ *Film Reviews*
- ❑ *Music Reviews (Concerts or Recordings)*
- ❑ *Travel (Weekend Getaways)*
- ❑ *Profiles on Advertisers*
- ❑ *Editorial/Opinion*
- ❑ *General Business*
- ❑ *The Latest Fads or Trends*

Advertising revenues are the life blood of these publications. If you can show that your writing will increase ad revenues, you have a job! If possible, write a short article (350 words) on a business you know the publication would love to have as an advertiser. If the article is entertaining and informativc, you have a good chance of getting it published.

The time-honored formula for crafting an article is the **5 W's**: *Who? What? When? Where?* and *Why?* Pick a subject and apply the 5 W's to it in sequence. You're off and running. Add a catchy title, an interesting beginning with a "grabber" of an opening sentence, easy-to-read body copy and a powerful ending. You now have an article worth reading.

If you cannot decide what to write about, put all your books in piles according to genre: *Romance, Music, Science Fiction, Adventure, Biography, Business, Travel,* etc. The largest stack will be the genre of most interest to you. You should be able to write in this genre with style and enthusiasm. Then find a category "fit" with a newspaper or magazine.

Strive to publish in more than one publication. If a

publication is unwilling to pay for your work, ask for ad space in exchange. In this way, you can advertise your services in any manner you choose. You can even barter with someone who has a product to sell by exchanging your ad space for cash.

Take a college writing class. Creative writing classes are a mainstay of many community colleges. Go to the library. Ask for *Writer's Digest* — a fine magazine that publishes articles that will teach you how to write and market your work. For more information, call *Writer's Digest* at 1-800-759-0963, or write to them at 1507 Dana Avenue, Cincinnati, Ohio 45207.

The Writer is another fine magazine that features tips from some of the world's greatest writers on how to write fiction and nonfiction. You can write to them at: *The Writer*, 120 Boylston Street, Boston, Massachusetts 02116.

Another good source for where and how to sell what you write is the *Writer's Market.* This writer's guide is published every year. It lists over 4,000 places to sell your work.

Most libraries carry these publications.

Tip #21: Learn to speak in front of groups.

As much as **85% of your career success** depends on how well you communicate with and relate to others. The ability to communicate forcefully and convincingly is the mark of an effective executive.

Public Speaking is one of life's most feared activities. In order to master the art of public speaking, you need to face and conquer this fear.

Volunteer to speak for local universities, libraries and community groups. Make it easy for yourself by giving a speech on a familiar topic.

Join Toastmasters or other public speaking organizations to improve your speaking ability. Consult the *Yellow Pages* to locate Toastmasters and other public speaking groups in your area.

When giving a speech, pay strict attention to Millard Bennet's five public speaking rules:

- ❑ *Arrest Attention*
- ❑ *Arouse Interest*
- ❑ *Create Desire*
- ❑ *Convince the Audience*
- ❑ *Get Favorable Action*

PART II. PERSONAL ORGANIZATION

The purpose of this section is to help you organize your life. Follow the tips outlined in this section, and you will improve your chances to earn the kind of salary you dream about.

"*If only there were 28 hours in a day, I'd get so much more done.*" Sound familiar? If you believe this statement is truc, I challenge you to change your mindset! If you organize your day well and manage your time with meticulous care, you will find "extra" hours in your day to do whatever you desire.

DOES ANYBODY REALLY KNOW WHAT TIME IT IS?

Here is an added tip to consider. If you are the type that sets his or her watch intentionally ahead to "trick" yourself, consider getting a *Xtraour Clock.* The Xtraour reduces each minute to 57.6 seconds giving you 25 hours in a day. The Xtraour is available at up-scale department stores.

When Seeking Employment:

Tip #22: Carefully prepare for interviews by organizing your thoughts.

You should:

a) ***Learn as much as you can about the company.*** You can find most of what you need to know at your local library. The most common sources of information are *Dun & Bradstreet, Standard and Poors Directory*, and *The Thomas Registry.*

b) ***Make a list of anticipated questions and prepare answers in advance.*** Your answers should be direct and succinct. Don't memorize pat answers or sound rehearsed; prepare fluid responses to broad questions. Be natural and totally honest.

Think before you answer...

Some interviewers will interrogate you like a prosecuting attorney. Don't be intimidated; stay relaxed and show grace under fire. Don't get flustered or fight back in desperation.

Here are some common interview questions or inquiries:

Tell me about yourself.
What is your main goal in life?
Why do you want to work for this company?
Describe your chief weaknesses —Your key strengths.
Why are you leaving your present job?
Why were you fired (or laid-off)?
What kind of salary are you expecting?
Where do you see yourself in 5 years?
What did you like least about your last job?

KILLER QUESTION

What is the your "second" best accomplishment?

Interviewers use this question to determine how quickly you "think on your feet." If an interviewer asks this question, you can be sure the next question will be, "What is your *most* outstanding accomplishment?"

Maintain a positive and stress-free attitude. Listen to the question intently; pause for a second or two to gather your thoughts, then respond. The slight pause tells the interviewer that you are the kind of person who thinks before you speak.

When unsure of the meaning of a question, ask the interviewer to repeat or clarify the question. Don't stray. Discuss only the facts pertinent to the question asked. Don't be baited by quickly answering loaded questions. "What did you like least about your last job?" has launched many a job applicant into an angry tirade against past employers and associates!

c) ***Close the interview and clinch the deal.*** Prepare a **scripted close** to end the interview on a high note. If you really want it, ask for the job!

Example: "I really like this company and feel I would make a significant contribution. If you hire me, I will give you 110%!"

When Employed:

Tip #23: Be a **Career Strategist**.

Organize your career objectives into a simplified, strategic plan. When putting together your career plan, observe the ***KISMIF*** principle: *Keep It Simple, Make it Fun!*

IF YOU FAIL TO PLAN, YOU PLAN TO FAIL

Have a vision of what you hope to accomplish, and make it part of your overall career mission. If you believe you can be the vice president of your company in five years, commit it to paper. Lay out the steps you need to take in order to achieve your vision. Establish specific time frames for attaining career goals. Include in your career plan when and how you expect to get promotions and raises.

Your career plan must include:

- ❑ A personal career vision.
- ❑ Career mission statement.
- ❑ Specific goals with predetermined time frames for accomplishment.
- ❑ A list of key tactics you will use.
- ❑ A support network (family, key associates, and resources).

A recent Harvard Business School study revealed that students who committed their goals to paper some 20 years earlier made more money and had more prestigious jobs than those students who did not commit their thoughts to paper.

MONO-MANIAC WITH A MISSION

General "*Stormin' Norman*" Schwarzkopf of Persian Gulf War fame never wavered from his goal of ousting Iraqi forces, thereby liberating Kuwait. While others pressed for the capture of Saddam Hussein and the taking of Baghdad, Schwarzkopf kept his focus. He knew exactly where he was going, and what tactics to use to accomplish his mission. You need to create the same single-mindedness within yourself when instituting your career plan.

Schwarzkopf also did his homework. Through a network of contacts, he gathered information about how people in the Middle East think — he knew the Middle Eastern Mind just as an employee should know the "mind" of his or her company.

The *Whole Career Sourcebook* by Robbie Miller Kaplan will help you establish your career plan. This book will show you how to identify career options, assess your skill-set, cultivate contacts and spot career and industry trends.

Tip #24: Organize your career plan into short-term, intermediate and long-term goals in the following areas.

- ❑ *A Major Definite Purpose*
- ❑ *Physical Fitness*
- ❑ *Job Titles & Promotions*
- ❑ *Additional Education*
- ❑ *Family, Leisure Time*
- ❑ *Self-Development*

List at least three goals in each category. Be specific, and be sure to include an action plan that outlines how you will go about achieving each goal. Describe the resources or skills you will use, and include the timing for attaining each goal.

Expect to achieve upward mobility in your career, but don't expect overnight success. During your first six months on a job, you will stumble around getting acclimated to your environment. During the next six months, you will learn what you are supposed to do. In the second year, you will "get good" at your job. In year three, expect to excel.

If this is the case with you, think twice about accepting that tempting promotion too soon. It may promote you to a level of incompetence. This is known as *The Peter Principle* and has destroyed many a fast-paced executive career.

Tip #25: Twenty five productivity "*killers*" that destroy effectiveness:

- ❑ Interruptions — unexpected visitors, meetings, etc.
- ❑ Telephone calls.
- ❑ Focusing on efficiency rather than effectiveness; efficiency is "*doing things right,*" while effectiveness is, "*doing the **right** things.*"
- ❑ Lack of focus — no mission or clear-cut objectives.
- ❑ Poor time management skills.

- ❑ Paperwork.
- ❑ Doing "busywork" — working "in" the business versus "on" the business.
- ❑ Procrastinating — not taking immediate action.
- ❑ Duplication of effort.
- ❑ Poor listening skills.
- ❑ Meetings, meetings, and more meetings!
- ❑ Lack of organization — jumping from one task to another.
- ❑ Relying on memory instead of writing it down.
- ❑ Lack of appropriate training.
- ❑ Poor management information system.
- ❑ Stress — on the job, and at home.
- ❑ Being stubborn only looking at things one way.
- ❑ Poor quality.
- ❑ Travel — commuting to and from work.
- ❑ Tardiness.
- ❑ Surrounding yourself with mediocre staff — doing everything yourself.
- ❑ Bringing personal problems to the office.
- ❑ Dwelling on conflicts without regard for resolution.
- ❑ Inadequate equipment or facilities.
- ❑ Crisis management or "firefighting."

One of the best ways to eliminate productivity killers is to take a time management course. One such course is *Time Management for Results* available through Brian Tracy Learning Systems (619) 481-2977.

Tip #26: Invest in a computer to increase your productivity.

Computers can help you handle home finances, school work and complex business problems. They can be used to log business contacts and schedule your work week. When investing in a computer, think long term. Buy a computer with sufficient memory and large enough hard drive (at least 20MB hard drive and 2M memory). Make sure the computer has enough memory for the software programs you want to run. Regardless of the make and model of the computer you choose, be sure it is compatible with either IBM or Macintosh.

Look into some of the new notebook computers. Most weigh under 7 pounds, and possess the power of larger computers. These attributes make notebook size computers perfect when traveling.

After you select computer hardware, it is time to choose the appropriate software. Here are some of my favorites:

- ❑ *Microsoft Word for Windows for word processing.*
- ❑ *Quicken for home finances.*
- ❑ *Grammatik for grammar checking.*
- ❑ *Act! for establishing a client or business associate database.*
- ❑ *Lotus 3.0 for spreadsheet capabilities.*

Stop by your local computer store and investigate the newest software programs on the market.

Learning word processing, Lotus and other menu driven programs will increase your productivity, reduce administrative burdens and provide you with professional looking reports (assuming you have a good printer). Once you master these programs and become computer literate, you will improve your time management and organizational skills.

USE IT, OR LOSE IT!

Be sure to use your computer. A computer should improve your productivity, not hinder it. Having a powerful computer at your disposal and not utilizing its capabilities is a waste of resources.

Remember the words of Robert Solow who stated, "*If someone landed from Mars-or, more to the point, from Tokyo-he'd unfortunately conclude in many cases, that the computer has had essentially no impact on our white collar productivity.*"

Tip #27: Invest in an inexpensive car phone, especially if you plan to work for yourself or embark on a career in sales.

A car phone can increase productivity and provide you with a competitive edge. Invest in Voice Mail for your car telephone. There is nothing more annoying than hearing a prerecorded voice say, "*Sorry, the mobile customer is away from the vehicle.*" Keep your incoming announcement short. Tell the caller they have 30 seconds to leave a message — if you give them unlimited message space, you are asking for trouble!

If you don't have a car, get a pager/beeper. Staying in touch with the office and getting back to important clients quickly is a sure sign of a caring and focused executive.

When considering a car phone, be sure to check public auctions and "out of business" sales. They can reap a bounty of office and communications equipment.

Don't overuse your car phone! Without realizing it, you can run up large bills rather quickly. Some business consultants and salespeople rack up bills in excess of $1,000 a month. Be selective when you give out your car phone number.

Use these four tips to lower your car phone bill:

a) Don't print your car telephone number on business cards and literature. Use your mobile telephone only as a business tool.

b) Give the number to only a few who have the presence of mind to know how to get their message across fast! Professionals will cut the conversations short because they are aware of the high costs involved.

c) Use your secretary as a clearinghouse for calls. Schedule it so your secretary can forward names and telephone numbers to you every hour on the hour. In this way you can screen your calls and immediately return calls to VIPs; the other calls get returned from the office.

d) Even the shrewdest business professional forgets THE PLATINUM CELLULAR TELEPHONE RULE: he or she is being charged for INCOMING CALLS! The incoming call is not only on the caller's "ticket," but on yours too. Keep incoming and outgoing calls under 2 minutes.

John Gill of L.A. Cellular, one of the nation's top purveyors of pagers and mobile telephones, echoes the above suggestions: "*Keep business calls strictly business. Don't use a car telephone for chatting with family and friends.*"

Tip #28: Set up a "suspense system" or follow-up file.

A suspense system file will help you keep track of tasks you have delegated, projects due, and general correspondence to be written or read.

You can use a simple 1 - 31 (days in a month) folder, or a computerized time management system. If you deal with many customers, invest in a software program like *ACT*. This program will help you keep track of important client follow-up calls and appointments. It will also remind you of things left undone.

Be certain to check your suspense system file *every* morning.

Tip #29: Keep a perfectly organized personal and business filing system.

Each file folder should be color coded according to topic and kept in chronological order. Keep files for general business, education, personal finances, taxes, important press clippings and articles, and reference materials. Always keep copies of presentations you have given for future reference.

One of the biggest time wasters is searching for something you have misplaced when you really need it. It pays to employ a part-or full-time administrative assistant to set up, organize and maintain a filing system.

A good source for an assistant is your local high school or community college. Leave your skill and salary requirements with the school's job counselor. You can even post an ad on the campus bulletin board. Besides filing chores, you will find your "student associate" of great value when faced with time-consuming jobs such as stapling, folding, inserting, photocopying and running administrative errands.

Tip #30: Invest in a daily planner to help you manage your time.

Comprehensive planners will assist you in managing priorities, setting client appointments, keeping track of travel expenses, and generally organizing your life.

Don't get into the habit of depending on memory to keep appointments. No matter how sharp your memory, you should put all appointments or promises to call in your planner.

What if I lose my daily planner? You can put the contents on a computer as a back-up. If you are like me and tend to scribble ideas and notes only you can decipher, it's wise to regularly photocopy the data contained in your daily planner in case you lose it. I keep so much of my career and life plans in my planner, I'd be lost without it.

An elaborate planner such as a *Geodex* can handle and organize every aspect of your life. I keep names, addresses, phone numbers, my daily schedule, my career plan, personal finances, investments and family photos in my Geodex.

When people see my Geodex, they often comment, *"I see that you use a Geodex. I never trust a business associate who doesn't use a planner/organizer."*

Planner Power

One of my favorite tactics is to let potential clients see my calendar pages booked months in advance. It shows them I'm in demand. This gives me an edge when negotiating consulting fees.

For more information about *Geodex*, call 1 - 800 - 833-3030.

Regardless of Your Employment Status:

Tip #31: Don't be a time waster!

Use normally unproductive time to your advantage. If you can turn *just 15 minutes per day* of unproductive time into productive time, you will positively affect your productivity. Turn this newly found productive time into earnings, and you will realize an instant increase in salary.

Consider this:

Most people waste over two hours per day watching mindless sitcoms, etc. The average American between the age of 16-24 spends over 22 hours per week watching television and 20 hours per week listening to the radio!

If you fit into this mold, you are wasting the chance to dramatically increase your earning power. If you can convert just half of this wasted time into earnings, you will increase your annual salary by thousands of dollars.

One of the biggest time wasters is travel. Traveling is one of the easiest ways to chew up productive time and create personal "downtime." When traveling by plane, train, or automobile, you waste hours just sitting.

To stimulate your thinking and create a learning environment, consider these few tips:

When traveling in a car, listen to *Talk Radio* to gain insight into world and local events. When traveling, listen to foreign language, instructional, motivational and self-improvement audiocassettes. Read for a change. Keep a pen, notepad and minicassette recorder handy to capture thoughts and ideas.

The Portable Office by Jefferson D. Bates will teach you how to decrease your personal downtime and get more done in airports, airplanes, cars and hotel rooms.

Caution: When driving a car, keep your eyes on the road!

ADDITIONAL TIME WASTERS

- ❑ The information age has created excessive paperwork. Employees spend up to 60% of their time processing paper.

- ❑ Most employees do not know how to control the processes in their sphere of influence.

- ❑ Many employees spend too much time working "***in***" (coping with the details of their work) the business, not "***on***" the business (long-term planning, creative thinking, spending time with clients, etc.).

- ❑ Interruptions. *The Center for Creative Leadership* claims the average uninterrupted time for managers or executives is only 14 minutes!

The Institute for Business Technology has an excellent training program called *PEP, (Personal Employee Productivity)* which deals with improving white collar productivity. You can reach them at (213) 550-6947.

Tip #32: Spend 15 minutes per week reflecting back on your accomplishments.

Keep a journal and analyze your actions. *Ask yourself:* What did I accomplish this week? What could I have done differently? What did I learn that I can put to immediate use? What opportunities surfaced on which I can capitalize?

Revisit your career plan. Create a positive state of mind and decide on the immediate actions to take to improve future results.

Tip #33: Be a *resource* and *information* hound!

Ask any management consultant how he or she is able to "switch hats" and provide a variety of services to clients. How can they analyze a management information system one day and conduct a strategic planning session the next?

Management consultants are, by necessity, problem solvers. To excel, they must be adept at gathering information and utilizing resources. Do not limit yourself in terms of the problems you tackle. Use the library, call experts familiar with the problem area, and attend training sessions targeting your problem.

How you gather information and tap into expert resources efficiently can be the deciding factor that places you heads above the competition.

Play a Game of Cards

Tip #34: Save those business cards!

People will give you their business cards for many reasons: to get rid of you, to play the numbers game (the more cards they give out, the better their chances of selling something), or they genuinely want to do business with you.

Immediately put the cards into a business card file or computerized name/address/phone number program. Many people find card files cumbersome. They find it easier to place business card data on computer files marked by category; e.g., computers, sales, executives, public relations, etc.

In time, you will create a powerful network resource data bank. Better yet, you will be able to retrieve the right person for the right job in record time.

PART III. IMAGE & PERCEPTIONS

Contrary to the maxim, people often do judge a book by its cover. The world revolves around perceptions. Perceptions outweigh reality in many cases.

Do you know that research shows tall, attractive people get promoted more often than their shorter, less attractive associates? Have you ever heard the expression, "He is a technician, not one for senior management"?

These statements emphasize that your image, and people's perception of it, will affect your career progress.

This section of the book will help you get rid of any misconceptions that may exist about you. You will learn the importance of personal groomimg, body language and the value of blending into a corporation's culture.

Regardless of Your Employment Status:

Tip #35: Dress for success.

Dress conservatively in well-tailored suits — dark blues or greys, shoes polished, conservative ties and a minimum number of accessories. Dressing for success will increase your self confidence during interviews, meetings and formal gatherings. Valmar Martin once said, "*Always dress so that if the big boss calls you into his/her office, you'll never be embarrassed.*"

Dress the Part, not like Art

Before you go on an important interview, take a good look in the mirror and check for these minor details:

- ❑ Men should be able to see the cuffs of their shirt just sticking out from the sleeves of the suit jacket.

- ❑ When wearing a tie, the length should be just below the top of your belt (men). Women wearing a tie should be sure it projects the "feeling" of power.

- ❑ Pants length should be just long enough to form a slight break just above the top of the ankle.
- ❑ Shirts should be pressed and have a conservative looking collar.
- ❑ Skirt lengths for women should be kept on the conservative side — not too short nor too revealing.
- ❑ Women should not wear heavy perfume or dangling, noisy jewelry.

What a Difference a Suit Makes

Dressing for success is an everyday affair. If you are unsure of the dress code, look to the chief representative of your corporate culture, the president or CEO. Imitate their style of dress.

Dressing appropriately and conservatively can be the difference between a good first impression and a bad one. Here's a personal story that brings this to light.

A few years ago, I did some work for a Big Six accounting firm. At one point, I needed to meet the senior partner to get his "blessing." Since this was not a formal interview, I did not heed my own advice.

There I was, dressed "to the nines" in my *Giorgio Armani* double-breasted suit and *Hugo Boss* tie. Sure, this stuff is top shelf, but I forgot to consider my audience. I met the senior partner in his office. He was dressed appropriately: single pleated dark blue suit, paisley tie and wingtip shoes! The partner didn't even stand up to shake my hand. Rejection was written all over his face — "*Hey pal, if you want to do business with us, get with the program.*"

Even though I got past the interview and continued to do work for this firm, I asked for another chance to talk with the partner. I wanted him to know I had some business savvy, and that I had made a big mistake.

I was granted a second meeting. This time I walked in wearing a dark blue "banker's" suit, a conservative tie and wingtip shoes (the exact style shoes he was wearing!). I got my hair cut, shaved 15 minutes before the meeting (portable razor) and polished my shoes while at the airport.

Although I can't say it made all the difference, I did receive a formal job offer soon after the meeting.

The lesson learned? Sometimes you have to...

Walk their walk, talk their talk, and wear their uniform.

To keep up on the latest fashion trends, read *Gentlemen's Quarterly* (men), *Working Woman* and *Executive Female* magazines.

Tip #36: Pay strict attention to personal grooming, particularly hair and nails.

Hair should be styled to conform to the corporate culture. Nails should be neat and clean. To this day, I don't understand why men are afraid of manicures. I continue to get compliments about how nice I keep my nails. Check out the CEO — believe me, he or she gets a manicure.

Women should keep their makeup natural looking. Men should shave closely and carry an electric razor for dealing with the *Five O'Clock Shadow.* Don't overdo it with strong colognes or perfumes!

Never underestimate the importance of personal grooming. Many job offers and promotions have been lost because the decision maker did not like the hairstyle of the person being interviewed. This is particularly true for men.

Tip #37: Stay physically fit.

Morning runs and daily workouts reduce stress. They also increase your energy level and give you the appearance of health and power. Drug and alcohol abuse are life and career suicide. Even the slightest reputation for recreational drug use or getting publicly drunk can mark you as an addict. Smoking is also becoming socially unacceptable and is often perceived as a sign of instability, dependence and weakness.

Try to avoid drinking during the business day. If a business lunch dictates "One Drink" to placate a client or higher-up, nurse it. If you don't drink, say so — and don't make excuses.

In even the most casual social setting, watch your alcohol consumption in the company of your peers. Refer to your corporate culture. There are companies and bosses who frown on any use of alcohol; others enjoy getting together after work to "bend some elbows."

If you must drink, set a limit. Keep your wits about you and do not drive! If you feel pressured to drink, say "*I'm giving my liver a vacation*" and order a soft drink. You can order a club soda with fruit juice, or nonalcoholic beer, wine or champagne. Refusing to smoke or drink is fast becoming a nonissue as companies faced with high Workman's Compensation Insurance and job stress lawsuits stand behind workers who eliminate "*liver aerobics.*"

THE GOLDEN GLOW OF POWER

Many top executives maintain a deep tan, even in winter. A good tan radiates strength and the *golden glow of power.* If your skin can tolerate it, visit a tanning salon where you can safely brown your skin. See if it makes a difference in how you are perceived. Check with your Doctor before undergoing any tanning treatment.

Health and physical fitness are standards of personal excellence in the 90s. Being physically fit enables you to work longer hours without fatigue, makes you more attractive and shows a high level of personal discipline. A quick game of racquetball at lunchtime will do wonders for your attitude and your waistline. Many employers have Wellness Incentive Programs to reward employees who stay in shape. Be sure to get a complete physical examination every few years.

Staying fit has side benefits. Gyms are great for networking. Many top executives start their day with a workout. It is common to find these VIP's at a 7 a.m. Aerobics class. Rubbing shoulders with them can help your career.

Tip #38: Learn to RELAX and cope with stress.

The 90s finds people divided into two groups: those worried about losing their jobs, "*When will the hammer fall?*" and those shouldering an increased workload as companies downsize to a minimum number of employees expected to maintain productivity.

Stress tolerance and proper stress management are signs of maturity. Learning new ways to cope with stress will enable you to think more clearly and be more productive. *Essi-Systems* of San Francisco, California has a comprehensive stress test available for under $20. The Essi-System test evaluates your stress level and pinpoints the source of the stress.

You can also purchase Biofeedback Stress Relief cards at most drugstores for a few dollars. These cards change color based on skin temperature to reveal your stress level. The cards come with printed material that outline simple stress relief exercises.

After testing and estimating your stress level, learn simple stress management techniques such as deep breathing and visualization to overcome the things that cause the stress.

Here is one powerful exercise to consider. Close your eyes while sitting in a comfortable position. Slowly count to 50, inhaling deeply through your nose and exhaling through your mouth. Envision placing annoying individuals or other stressors in a cloud above your head. At the right moment (when you're feeling relaxed), trigger an explosion and *blow them to smithereens!*

Another technique is writing the name of the stress-causing individuals on the bottom of your shoes. Stomp around a little and crush them to *insignificance!*

If you are being hassled by someone who makes your blood pressure rise, visualize them as being two feet tall and wearing a red clown nose.

People can cause stress *only* if you allow them.

USING THE RIGHT FORK

Tip #39: Improve your table manners and etiquette.

The book, *Leticia Baldridge's Executive Manners*, is a fine teacher of these essentials. Learn how to order a wide variety of ethnic foods and fine wines.

How you conduct yourself at business lunches and company dinner parties will be the gauge of your class, style and maturity.

I remember an incident where not knowing which fork to use cast a shadow of doubt on a young executive being considered for a high level promotion. The top executive figured that if this manager did not possess social graces, he probably could not mingle appropriately with the top brass.

Tip #40: Maintain eye contact when speaking to others.

Strong eye contact gives an air of confidence, as long as you don't participate in a "stare down." Break off eye contact intermittently. Smile, be enthusiastic and display intense interest in what the other person has to say — nod frequently, and don't glower!

KNOW YOUR AUDIENCE

In some cultures, extended periods of eye contact are considered rude and disrespectful. In the Korean culture, for example, looking directly into the eyes of an *elder* is considered challenging and somewhat disrespectful.

Senior management may use intense eye contact in an attempt to intimidate you. Don't be cowed — hold your ground and maintain eye contact until you start to feel uncomfortable. Change the subject, tell a joke, anything to break the starer's concentration.

Some people speak fast in order to dominate conversations. Learn to speak less and listen more. People who speak less and listen more are perceived to be more intelligent, trustworthy and empathetic.

Tip #41: Perform a monthly Positive Attitude Adjustment.

Reflect back on your successes and failures. Rid yourself of all the things — people, attitudes and obstacles — that stand in your way. Ask yourself:

What can I do right NOW to improve my attitude and increase my enthusiasm?

Enthusiasm is infectious. Enthusiastic people exude drive, energy and excitement. Your positive attitude will filter down to your team and co-workers. When people are "*Fired-Up!*" amazing things happen!

Tip #42: Keep your sense of humor.

You know the old saying, "*If I wasn't laughing about it, I'd be crying*." Read the newspaper's comic section daily. Go to comedy clubs. Watch comedy shows on HBO, SHOWTIME and ARTS & ENTERTAINMENT. Buy a joke book and memorize a few tales to tell friends. Associate with people who make you laugh.

Stuff happens! Why sweat the things you cannot change? Laughter is the best cure for disappointment. Situations that can't be changed won't be, so you may as well accept them. A sense of humor and quick wit will put you in the right frame of mind to deal with almost anything that crops up.

As you climb the rungs of the corporate ladder, things will not go exactly as you planned. Humor can be more than a stress reliever; it's a good way to put you in a creative mood. Behind all humor is a core of seriousness. Your wildest and craziest thoughts can generate the most successful ideas!

Tip #43: Polish your writing skills.

Go to your local library or bookstore and seek out books with "How to write" themes. There are many good books available to improve your writing. One such book is *The Art of Readable Writing* by Rudolph Flesch; another is *Secrets of Successful Writing* by DeWitt Scott.

There are also seminars you can attend to improve your writing. Newspapers list seminars of this type in their calendar sections. Check with your local community college for classes. Another good source is *The American Management Association* (located in New York).

If you have a computer and would like to improve your writing, there is no better investment than the *Grammatik* program. *Grammatik* will show you how to improve your grammar, spelling, and ability to craft sentences.

THE WRITER'S NIGHTMARE

Have you ever heard of writer's block? This usually happens when writers are under pressure to meet deadlines. They draw a blank, conjuring up the nightmare that their creative pool has dried up!

Writers tend to get stuck on opening sentences. Here are three ways to overcome writer's block:

1. When trying to come up with an appropriate beginning, stimulate your thought process by pondering the phrase, "*I'd like to tell you that . . .*" Envision yourself talking to your audience. Finish the phrase, ***"I'd like to tell you that . . ."*** with the message you are trying to convey.

2. As you write, ask these questions:

- ❑ What is ***it*** that I am trying to say?
- ❑ Why is this topic **important**?
- ❑ What are the **benefits** of this topic?
- ❑ What are the **how-to's** involved?

3. Skip the beginning. Write "the rest" and then go back and write the opening.

Good writing skills are imperative as you move up the corporate ladder. People will judge your intellect, education and your common sense when reading something you have written.

Tip #44: Learn a second, if not a third, language.

As our economy becomes more global in nature, bilingual skills will become a prerequisite for certain types of employment. Knowing how to communicate in two or three languages increases your chances for promotion.

Japanese, Chinese, Russian and Arabic are good language choices. For a perspective view, only a few hundred million people in the world speak English (out of over 5.5 billion people worldwide). With the coming of a *United European Market,* being able to converse in French and German will be valuable. An ability to converse in Spanish will set you apart in light of free trade agreements with Mexico and the exploding Hispanic population in the United States. Decide which of these languages will help you in your career. Take a college course in the language of your choice.

Mastering a foreign language is only part of the equation as being familiar with foreign customs and business practices is of equal importance (See ***Tip #60***).

When representing your company overseas, you will find it easier to do business if you're sanctioned as being "OK!" by citizens of that country. To achieve this end, join a club with members of your chosen foreign language to hone your language skills. Make long-term friendships and get letters of introduction.

Many cultural clubs have chapters at certain universities. If you cannot locate a club, contact the country's consulate located in your state's largest city. They will be able to refer you to the club nearest you. It isn't necessary to master your chosen language, but you should be competent in basic conversational skills.

Tip #45: Increase your vocabulary.

Your intelligence and education are often gauged by how you use words and structure sentences. Books such as *Word Power* and audiocassette tapes like *Verbal Advantage* are invaluable tools for increasing your vocabulary.

The English language is horribly underused. The average English speaking person uses anywhere from 800 - 1,000 words out of over 200,000 words in the English lexicon!

FOR NORM CROSBYS ONLY

I know a person who frequently and unintentionally fractures the English language. He sounds uneducated. He once confused the word *coronary* with the word **corollary** and embarrassed himself in front of his peers.

Unless you possess the word command of Norman Mailer or William F. Buckley, don't use a ten dollar word when a one dollar word will do. Learn to speak to the level of your audience. Forget big words if you don't have a grasp of their meaning or usage. In your quest to appear smarter than the "average bear," you may become a laughing stock.

Tip #46: Learn the art and science of body language and the power of nonverbal communication.

A person's stance, posture and facial expressions can tell you what he or she is thinking, or at least implying. For example, when people sit back in their chairs and fold their arms, it usually signifies a defensive posture suggesting disagreement or doubt. When the same people sit forward in their chairs and gesture by showing you the palms of their hands, it suggests accord and agreement.

One good start in communicating confident body language is posture — don't slouch or appear round shouldered. Like Mom use to say, "*Stand up straight!*"

There are many good books available on body language and nonverbal communication such as Ken Cooper's *Body Language* available in most bookstores. This book explores the human idiosyncrasies associated with silent communication, and also explains how to interpret different human actions.

Tip #47: Learn to understand the differences in the ways men and women communicate.

Research shows that men and women say the same things in a slightly different way. Women tend to be intuitive and expressive; men, on the other hand, tend to be logical and direct. Understanding subtle gender communication differences will help you work better in groups and prevent you from prejudging situations. The book, *You Just Don't Understand* by Deborah Tannen, will help you understand these subtle gender communication differences.

Tip #48: Understand the meaning of a Psychological Contract, or *Psychon.*

According to Dr. Herb Baker, a Psychon is "*The sum total of all written and unwritten, spoken and unspoken, realized and unrealized, expectations held by the parties in any interaction.*"

Psychological contracts begin during the initial job interview. The employer and prospective employee negotiate terms — some directly stated, some implied and some unspoken. Be sure to get all your expectations in writing to clear up any confusion.

During the honeymoon period, or first 30 days on the job, uncover your company's unspoken expectations and norms not explained in the policy manual. It may be participation in the company's pet charity, or a certain mode of dress. The boss may not like Liberal Democrats, the Los Angeles Raiders or brown suits — so people avoid mentioning them.

A company norm may be to work late, an hour past quitting time. You need to be aware of these unspoken expectations. A long standing employee or human resource manager can give you a rundown on these unwritten expectations. You may be the most productive worker in your company, but if you bolt for the parking lot at 5 p.m. you may lose that promotion to someone less qualified who stays an hour past quitting time (the boss just hates clock watchers).

Tip #49: When considering a career change, perform a *Personal Skills Inventory*.

This inventory should include:

- ❏ *Significant Skills*: What is your major talent? Writing? Speaking? Sales? Mathematics? Marketing Analysis? Training? Ask yourself: "What do I really like to do? What do I do best?"

- ❏ *Key Personality Traits*: Are you a people person, or a behind-the-scenes type? Do you value mass production over hand craftsmanship, or vice versa? Are you a positive, relaxed and enthusiastic self-starter immune to the pressures of a fast-paced, rapidly changing environment? Or are you a controlled, highly organized, task-oriented worker bee who demands a structured, strictly supervised environment? (See ***Tip #16***).

- ❑ *Career Choices*: After listing your skills and key character traits, determine a number of possible career choices that match your skill-set. If you are a good problem solver and have excellent sales and interpersonal skills, consider the field of consulting. On the other hand, let's say you are a studious person with a strong interest in health and nutrition, a career in Chiropractic and Preventative Medicine is for you.

Use your best judgment. Solicit the advice of college professors and career counselors when completing the career possibility section of your inventory. When you have completed the list of possible careers, seek out additional training in the targeted areas.

The fields that are "safe bets"? Engineering (except Aerospace or Defense), Computers and Sales top the list. Science, Mathematics and Engineering will be fertile fields for job seekers for the next 20 years. In 1995, the United States will need an additional 300,000 high school math and science teachers.

By the year 2000, women and minorities will comprise over 75% of new hires. Most will not seek posts in science and engineering. By 2010, the combination of fewer college students majoring in science and engineering, plus the attrition of currently employed scientists reaching retirement age, means that American businesses will face an estimated shortage of 500,000 scientists.

According to a variety of respected sources outlined in *U.S. News & World Report*, here are the "Hot Tracks" in the Top Professions for the 90s:

- ◆ ***Computers***: Computer Aided Design Drafting. Numerical Controls Programmer. CAD/CAM Drill &

Lathe Machinist. Junior and Senior Computer Systems Analyst. Computer Security Administrator. Specialized Applications Programmer.

- ***Sales***: Domestic and International Product Marketing & Management for Consumer Products. International Marketers and Telemarketing Specialists.

- ***Health Care***: Immunology and Infectious Disease Control. Microbiologist. Pharmacologist. Public Health Doctor. Paramedics and Physician Assistants. Hospital Managers working with Medical Technologists and Consultants who negotiate discounts with Physicians in exchange for directing company employees their way for treatment.

- ***Nursing***: Licensed Practical Nurse, Registered Nurse and Head Nurse. Nurse-anesthetist. Community Health Professional. Corporate Nurse. Midwife.

- ***Financial***: Financial Product Sales for mutual fund families, financial planning firms, banks with discount brokerages and insurance companies. Tax Analyst and Financial Planner. Tax Accountant, Auditor, Cost Accountant and Forensic Accountant to deal with the bankruptcy, security fraud and financial schemes.

- ***Science***: Scientific Research for Chemical Engineers, specifically Materials Chemistry. Jobs are booming in this sector as chemists search to build better quality products that last. In medicine, to duplicate *Taxol*, the cancer-fighting substance produced by the rare California Yew tree; in manufacturing, to develop the light, fuel-efficient ceramic engine or fabrics that change color when exposed to sunlight.

- ***Telecommunications***: Network Management. Electrical Engineers with management skills who can keep fleets of technicians and engineers organized and maintaining valuable telecommunication networks. Communications Project Engineer.

- ***Architecture***: Architects specializing in Health Design Architecture and Historic Preservation.

- ***Education***: Education Program and Teacher Effectiveness Assessment Specialists. Educational Statistician. Trainers who can guide schools in administering and scoring tests.

- ***Engineering***: Electronic and Industrial Engineers who have marketing and sales ability in areas as diverse as cordless phones, industrial robots and advanced computer design. Environmental, manufacturing and mechanical design engineers who can communicate the benefits of high-tech products to potential customers.

- ***Environmental Management***: Industrial Hygiene. Anyone with skills in the area of dealing with toxic, hazardous waste and finding ways to reduce the negative impact of these materials upon employers, consumers and the environment. Asbestos Abatement Technologist. Chemical Risk Assessor.

- ***Credit Specialist***: Loan Workout Officer to deal with restructuring or "working out" delinquent loans. Business Development Officer. Regulation Compliance Officer. Credit and Collections Representative.

- ***Food Service and Distribution Management***: This area will grow in importance as the population "greys." Senior citizens must be fed at home, in nursing homes and in community centers.

- ***Human Resources and Diversity Management***: With the work force becoming more multiethnic, Cultural Diversity Managers are in demand. These workers will be asked to understand ethnic values, be sensitive to ethnic differences and to help minorities reach senior management. Training and Development Specialist. Compensation Specialist and Equal Employment Opportunity Representatives.

- ***Insurance***: Environmental claims specialist. Actuary, Underwriter and Employee Benefits Specialist.

- ***Law***: Environmental Lawyer and Corporate Bankruptcy Lawyer.

Generalized career choice videos are available through *Career Publishing* of Orange, California (800) 854-4014. If a career in politics interests you, the Career Publishing *Success Video Series* on this subject focuses on a cross-section of three major levels of government.

When you have learned everything you can about your *Career Choice,* then, and only then, should you venture out on interviews.

When Employed:

Tip #50: Execute a personal growth campaign.

Solicit feedback from your supervisor on a quarterly basis. Ferret out the objective and subjective criteria used to evaluate your performance; e.g., attitude, productivity, cost control, initiative, teamwork, etc. Know exactly what is expected of you and the time frame in which you are expected to complete tasks. Ask your supervisor how you are being perceived by co-workers and upper management.

Request a formal list of 90-day goals to be discussed during the next feedback session. These goals should consist of quantitative and qualitative objectives affecting your career growth. Organize these goals into a workable plan for improvement. Put them into action. You should also develop a plan to correct any perception problems that exist.

Learn to see yourself through the *eyes of others.*

REMEMBER: ***Perception is the editor of reality!***

THE PLAY'S THE THING

Tip #51: See intellectually stimulating plays and films on a regular basis.

Do not exclude foreign films or plays from your list. They will provide you with a different perspective on life and give you creative insight into life's daily problems and concerns.

Carefully observe the role playing that takes place during these performances. Evaluate the body language, psychology and motivations of the actors. This will show you how to read the nuances of language, the real *words* beneath the words.

Senior management will appreciate your ability to converse on a variety of topics, including the hottest films and plays.

Tip #52: Give it a rest!

Know when to quit to prevent burn-out. Some people are hellfire and flash at the starting line, only to poop out mid-race and fizzle at the finish line. Realistic types pace themselves in preparation for the long haul to produce consistent results.

At times your job will get to you — and it will show. You will exude a form of "*Mental Body Odor*" that will be a "downer" for all those who come in contact with you. An outward show of disenchantment is unproductive. It can cause others to question your health and fitness for promotion.

HERE TODAY, GONE TO-MAUI

It's not always possible to go on extended vacations. Weekend getaways are sure cures for job burn-out, so are mid-week getaways — less crowded, too! Vacations are for getting away from it all — that means leaving work and frustrations behind.

Pampering is not a dirty word. Men can learn a trick from women on how to deal with stress. While men reach for a drink, a "*Bracer*," women treat themselves to a hot bath or a massage. If money is no object, they will go to the beauty salon for the day. Then they shop 'till they drop.

Guys, it's OK to pamper yourself. Get a massage, manicure, pedicure and steam bath. Make yourself a new person, better able to deal with old problems.

Tip #53: Select a Role Model, and find a Mentor.

Observe and emulate successful people by mirroring their principles, philosophies and general attitudes. Pay close attention to how they treat those around them.

BE AS THEY ARE, NOT ONLY AS THEY DO

Study their vocabulary, their tone of voice and how they phrase words to influence others. Evaluate their ability to gather and make effective use of information. Mimic or mirror their walk, posture and confidence to duplicate their overall charismatic package.

SUCCESS BY ASSOCIATION

Mirroring winners is the quickest way to trigger success. To paraphrase famed boxing promoter Don King, "*I believe in success by association. In prison, if you associate with expert thieves, you will become an expert thief.*" When asked how he planned to become the first African-American billionaire, King replied, "*I associate with billionaires.*"

Mirroring success creates success! Tony Robbins of *Personal Power* fame offers excellent audiocassette tapes to teach you the techniques of Neurolinguistic Programming (NLP) and Mirroring. NLP is the repetition of key words and phrases calculated to create a successful mindset in yourself and others. Mirroring is a technique whereby you mimic the body language and posture of the person you are speaking with to create a favorable image (a mirror image of themself looking in a mirror).

FOLLOW THE LEADER

Great leaders take their cue from other great leaders. They are notorious for reading and studying about great leaders of the past. General George Patton studied the battle tactics of ancient cultures and created strategies for his armored divisions that mirrored the winning war campaigns of ancient Sparta, Rome and France. He used what he learned to defeat Rommel during World War II.

Go to the library and select six biographies of people who have made a positive mark on society in the past 50 years. Choose people you want to be like. Over the next three months, analyze the lives of your six Role Models. Select the factors or keys to success you want to emulate, whether it is their perseverance, integrity, dedication, or creativity.

Next, find a Mentor among the people in your sphere of influence who most exemplifies the character traits you targeted. Make an appointment to see him or her and establish a rapport. Reveal your intention to use them as a

Role Model. Explain that you feel success follows success. Determine if they are interested in nurturing your career. There's always the chance they don't have the time to participate in your growth. If they don't have the time, continue your search.

My book *Passionate Leadership: Ten Powerful Principles That Will Change Your Life!* (Delta Sales, 1-800-393-9737) contains a wealth of information on how to find and develop a lifetime relationship with a Mentor.

A Mentor relationship is far different from a Role Model relationship. A Role Model relationship can be conducted from afar; a Mentor is a respected friend and ally willing to give his or her time to coach you towards success. A true Mentor can forecast how you will react in certain situations, offer solutions and will always look out for your best interests.

Tip #54: When making a major business decision, consider the impact the decision has on the *Six Personal Values* deemed critical by United States corporations.

- ❑ Economic impact of the decision — what are the cost/benefits?

- ❑ Political implications — will the decision ruffle any feathers?

- ❑ Theoretical acceptance — does the decision agree with company-accepted practices?

- ❑ Religious significance — any religious overtones that could negatively affect the company image?

- ❑ Aesthetic appeal — how will the decision be perceived by the public and media?

- ❑ Social significance — will the decision help the community? Will the decision affect the environment or any special-interest group?

Tip #55: Come to grips with this reality: Many American corporations are uncomfortable with individuality.

They are like Japanese companies who treasure group consensus over individuality. The Japanese have a saying, "*The nail that sticks up will be pounded down.*"

Many corporations want their people to "get with the program." This simply means you need to understand the "heartbeat" and cultural aspects of your company in order to get ahead. I am not suggesting that *all* corporations want a bunch of clones working for them; I am saying that each company has a thriving, living, breathing culture that is part of the company success profile.

Get to know the company culture. Observe the way people dress. What kind of attire and demeanor is considered appropriate? Look at the shape and color of the corporate building. Does the color or shape of the corporate building stand for anything? What would you think about a black building with no windows? It would certainly tell you a few things about the company's culture.

Review company-sponsored slogans to understand the current company theme or mindset. It should give you some insight into how the company treats its people.

Does the company assign parking spaces only to top management? Are the personalities of top management conducive to a harmonious work atmosphere? What formal incentive programs does the company have in place?

Understanding the corporate culture will help you "fit in." Unless you flow with the tide of your company culture, you will create unnecessary opposition and make your ideas hard to implement. You will ultimately become an outsider who is politically ineffective (refer to ***Tip # 54*** and review how *Six Personal Values* impact corporate cultures).

Does this mean you have to become a robotic geek to survive? No, but it does mean you need to be self-aware.

RIDDLE: How can a corporation have a heart, when it has no soul?

There is a story of an executive who battled his company for months over minor issues. One day the executive marched into the president's office and turned in two weeks notice because he had found a better, higher paying job. He also knew the company's penchant for giving the dreaded *pink slip* to employees on Friday afternoons. They would order fired employees to clean out their desks, and worse, give them no severance pay.

The company president exploded. "Two weeks notice! It's unfair! It's not enough time to replace you!"

"*Tell me*," the executive replied with a smile. "*How many weeks would have given me had you fired me?*"

Tip #56: Don't burn bridges!

When you resign or are fired from a company, maintain a professional demeanor. Know when it's time to leave. Be prepared. Never resign unless you have a new job. Resigning without a firm job prospect leaves you without a bargaining chip and considerably weakens your worth in the marketplace.

Let's say you get an offer from a company you can't refuse. It's unwise to force your company into a bidding war. When the salary and position are right, go. Don't look back.

Senior management will view a bidding war as a form of blackmail. They may or may not accede to your demands. If they knuckle under, there's a good chance they will search for a replacement and fire you six months down the road. ***Tit for tat!***

If you are fired or laid-off, keep your composure. Don't get too emotional, because anger will cloud your judgment. No anger or retribution — when you badmouth others, you badmouth yourself! Should you be unexpectedly laid-off, many companies will give you full use of their facilities for 60 to 90 days — telephone, office, secretary — you can have the aura of employment as you search for a new job.

When laying off personnel, many companies offer severance pay and separation packages. If you lose your cool, you risk losing a severance package and may be labeled a troublemaker. This reputation will "dog" you throughout your career.

If you are fired or if you are just plain fed up and quit, leave with dignity, integrity and a list of future contacts — no temper tantrums, door slamming, or shouting matches.

Don't plan a quick departure. It is unprofessional to leave an employer, even a bad one, in the lurch. When the time comes for you to resign, plan a graceful step-by-step exit. Future employers will expect the same from you.

Write a polite letter stating your reasons for resigning. Thank your supervisor for the growth you experienced and friendships made during your employment.

Remember, your ex-employer is always in the driver's seat; ex-employers are like credit bureaus — they can do more damage to you, far more than you can ever do to them.

Tip #57: Invest in a home telephone answering machine or paging system.

If you expect an important call at home, you can call forward your home number to your pager and hit the road.

Missing important messages, especially emergency calls from senior managers, can label you as unreliable and adversely affect your career.

An answering machine and satellite pager will enable you to network more effectively. If your company has voice mail, participate in the program. Voice mail will improve your productivity and dramatically enhance interdepartmental communications. You will be able to leave a message for many people at the same time. Some people consider voice mail to be impersonal, so be careful not to abuse this form of communication.

Tip #58: Don't forget the small stuff!

Little things mean a lot. Always carry enough cash with you in case you get stuck paying for lunch or parking. Keep your car clean at all times. You never know when you'll be asked to drive a senior manager to the airport, or pick up an important client at a hotel. When driving, get directions in advance so you appear to have everything under control.

Use credit cards wisely. Credit card companies have begun to issue cards to college graduates. In turn, students who cannot find jobs are "living on the card" and in the hole for thousands of dollars. Use your cards only when you can pay the balance each month, otherwise you will end up in a situation similar to the federal deficit; you'll be paying out more than you're bringing in. Your payments will pay the interest while your debt, the principle, gets only slightly smaller each month.

These common sense suggestions may seem trivial, but you can bet that many young executives have been judged harshly for missing these minor details.

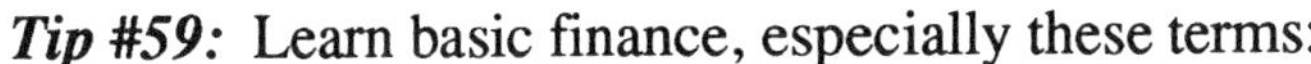

Tip #59: Learn basic finance, especially these terms:

- *Return On Investment* (***ROI***).
- *Return On Assets Employed* (***ROAE***).
- *Return on Equity* (***ROE***).
- *Net Present Value* (***NPV***).

Understanding these and other financial terms will help you recognize the key leverage points that drive economic business decisions. CEO's live and die by these economic indicators — so do the shareholders.

To learn about finance, take a course at a local college or attend a training seminar. The American Management Association has an excellent study-at-home program called, *Finance and Accounting for Nonfinancial Managers.* This audiocassette and workbook program will teach you everyday financial terms and how to read and interpret financial statements, balance sheets and managerial accounting reports. To order, call (518) 891-5510.

Two good reference quides for understanding finance are *The Vest Pocket MBA* and *The Vest Pocket CEO* — Prentice Hall publications available in most bookstores. They are excellent sources for financial formulas and key explanations of financial terms.

IGNORANCE IS BLISS

Tip #60: Learn how to conduct business with other cultures.

The "*Ugly American*" image prevails because the average American is language and world ignorant. Just ask one of your friends or family members to name a province in Canada. See what answer you get.

Did you know that Albertville, Alabama was bombarded with requests for 1992 Olympic Games tickets (instead of Albertville, France)?

Of all cultures, Americans rank at the bottom when it comes to bilingual skills. The Japanese ***demand*** that students learn a second language, preferably English.

Conducting business in a foreign country is quite different from doing business in the United States. Customs not only vary, but expressions and body language mean different things in other cultures.

In the Middle East, for example, you never show your host the soles of your shoes, pass papers with your left hand, decline hospitality like an offer of tea, or ask a person about their spouse before conducting business.

The Japanese are known to say *yes* when they mean ***no***. They smile to express sorrow, and laugh to display shock.

IT'S TIME TO PRACTICE JAPANESE

Japan is global powerhouse. The Japanese language will become very important as more American businesses expand to the Pacific Rim.

Language and customs go hand-in-hand. Go to a sushi bar on a slow night and yack it up with the Utamae-san (sushi chef) — they love to talk. Practice rudimentary Japanese. The restaurant's staff will appreciate your respect of the Japanese language and help you correct subtle nuances in phrasing. In time, you will sound like a native.

Two insightful books dealing with the Japanese on a business and cultural level are *Japanese Business Etiquette* by Diana Rowland and *Doing Business With The Japanese* by Mitchell F. Deutsch.

There is a wealth of information on video, audiocassette and in print, to help you better understand the inner workings of foreign cultures. Contact The State Department, the Transcultural Services Bureau and Intercultural Relations Institute for more information. These organizations are located in Washington D.C. but you can find a foreign consulate right in your state capitol or largest city.

The library is another good source for foreign cultural information (check the reference section). You can even take a course in International Business at a local university. One such course is *Trends In World Technology*, offered by San Diego's United States International University (USIU).

"Those who fail to plan, plan to fail!"

PART IV. PERSONAL "EDGE" TECHNIQUES

A horse that "wins by a nose" in the Kentucky Derby can earn ten times more money than the second place horse. The difference between a world class sprinter and an "average" track star is just one second. A golf pro can consistently win by being only two strokes better than the competition.

In each case, what separated the winners from the losers was a slight "edge." This section provides you with tips that will set you apart from others and give you this edge.

Remember the words of Paul Meyer: "*If you do a little bit more than average, from that point on your progress multiplies itself out of all proportion to the effort put in.*"

When Seeking Employment:

Tip #61: Find your ***Passion** in Life!*

"*Passion is the 5 a.m. rocket booster that bolts you out of bed each morning into your life's work with a vengeance.*" Passion is a burning sense of purpose that propels you to new heights of achievement.

Ask yourself: What do I love to do? What feelings, emotions and character traits emerge when I do the things I enjoy most?

If you absolutely love to play golf — how do you feel each time you swing a club and hit the ball straight, long and accurately? What resources do you call upon to play the game? Create the same mindset each time you need to be at your best.

By recreating the same frame of mind, you will have no problem feeling passionate about everything you do. You will bolt out of bed every morning anxious to start the day.

Three sources for learning how to find and develop your passion are:

1. My book, *Passionate Leadership: Ten Powerful Principles That Will Change Your Life!* available through Delta Sales Publishing at (800) 393-9737. If you are not passionate about your job, it's time to change fields and propel yourself to the top!

Here is my measure of a person's passion for life — if you hit the snooze button on your alarm clock more than once each morning, it's time to change careers.

2. Dr. David Viscott, the nationally syndicated TV and radio psychiatrist, conducts a seminar entitled *Finding Your Life's Passion.* You can learn more about this seminar or order the audiocassette version, by contacting the Viscott Institute in Beverly Hills, California.

3. Motivational speaker Tony Robbins, author of *Personal Power*, has a series of audiocassette tapes and books dealing with maximizing your passion quotient.

Tip #62: Create a *Personal Breakthrough Strategy.*

This strategy will ensure your long term career success. The key to a breakthrough strategy is identifying your uniqueness. The main question behind the strategy is, "*How can I position myself in the job market in a way that makes my talents unique?*"

Ask, and answer, these ten questions:

1. What can I offer an employer that others are not offering?

2. How can I save money for companies? Is there a particular skill I "bring to the table" that breeds efficiency?

3. How can I create a job that is fun, challenging and never boring?

4. What is my job market niche?

5. What would people pay for that isn't now available?

6. What trends could shape things to come?

7. How can I reposition an existing product to add value? Can I reshape or repackage it? What if I change the color? What if I market it to a different group?

8. What can I do to improve the convenience and affordability of a product or service?

9. How can I make an indelible mark on my industry or society in general?

10. What *one* thing can I do **RIGHT NOW** to make a difference!

Tip #63: Target an attractive position that is in demand.

According to *Money Magazine* (February, 1992), here are the average annual salaries of jobs that pay the most.

- ❑ Physician/Senior Practitioner - $315,000
- ❑ Financial Planner - $144,935
- ❑ Dentist - $116,550
- ❑ Veterinarian - $107,670
- ❑ Airline Pilot - $107,071
- ❑ Stock Broker - $106,493
- ❑ Lawyer - $105,628
- ❑ Lobbyist - $89,000
- ❑ Ad Executive - $83,290
- ❑ Purchasing Manager - $82,886

Also mentioned as top jobs were Aeronautical Engineer, Bank Officer and Biologist. The worst job? Taxi driver. The salary is average, the rewards practically nil.

How about growth? The jobs expected to grow in number more than 50% by the year 2025 are:

- ❑ Legal Assistant.
- ❑ Computer Analyst.
- ❑ Physical Therapist.
- ❑ Psychologist.
- ❑ Travel Agent.

Tip #64: Learn about a prospective employer before accepting a job.

Do your "homework." Verify the company's financial health and credit rating. Go to the library and secure business periodicals. Ask the librarian to provide you with as much information as possible; e.g., newspapers, trade journals, industry newsletters, etc.

Avoid companies with poor credit ratings. This usually indicates financial instability. Has the company lost any major contracts recently? Have there been any recent layoffs or mergers?

Vendors and suppliers are a good source of information. They work closely with companies on a day-to-day basis and are a good gauge of how companies pay their bills. Vendors can help you separate the good guys from the bad guys.

Don't rely on company size as an indicator of financial stability. Security Pacific National Bank was thought to be unassailable until it was roped by Bank of America. Even General Motors and IBM have had terrible performance records the past few years.

When Employed:

Tip #65: Twenty rules for keeping your job:

1. Get off to a strong start. Get to the office early and put in extra hours. This shows initiative and enthusiasm.

2. Follow the rules. You have to learn the rules before you can bend — or break — them! Refer to your company's operations manual. You may find that you have more freedom to act than you previously thought.

3. Keep a learning attitude. Don't be afraid to ask "*How?*" "*Why?*" and "*What's stopping us?*" Speak publicly and often of your commitment to education. Go for your MBA (See ***Tip #88***) and continue your education beyond your degree. In the area of technology, for example, there is always a need to stay abreast of rapidly changing developments. Be sure to keep your Personnel Department's file updated — your current level of education will have a bearing on future promotions.

4. Ferret out what senior management expects of you. What is really important to the powers that be? What are the measures and performance standards that senior management demands?

5. Be a team player. Don't be a renegade or loose cannon. Strive for workplace harmony. People have been fired or demoted for their inability to work well with "teammates."

6. *Save* your company money. Take on projects that eliminate waste and reduce expenses. Finish projects and tasks on time, under budget and to the best of your ability. Get the reputation of a *streamliner*, one of the traits associated with top CEOs.

7. Be decisive, a self-starter. Companies want employees that take initiative and are aggressive at getting results.

8. Use the telephone properly. Return calls promptly. Never answer the telephone with a joke, sarcastic remark or angry tone of voice. Keep personal calls to a minimum. Get a phone charge card and charge personal calls to it.

Don't give out too much information when handling your boss's calls. To say "He's away from his desk for the moment" is better than "Yeh, can you believe it? It's 3 p.m. and Joe's working on his fifth martini at lunch!"

Recommendation: Watch the video, *Make the Phone Work for You*, available through Communication Publications & Resources (800) 888-2086. This video will teach you how to make the telephone a powerful tool.

9. Plan your work daily and set departmental priorities each month. Create strategies for success. Solve problems before they come to the attention of senior management.

10. Don't be a troublemaker. No one, especially senior management, wants to hear you complain about others. Strive to become known for your straight talk and excellent management style.

11. Challenge yourself. Volunteer for the toughest jobs in your department. Not only will you gain a "clutch player" reputation, but you will be known as someone who loves a challenge.

HEARD IT THROUGH THE GRAPEVINE

12. Beware of the company grapevine. Report good and bad news to senior management. Do it promptly. If peers and senior management think you are hiding problems or behaving contrary to the aims of the company, the obvious question is, "What else are you covering up?"

13. Be loyal to others and true to yourself — enough said!

14. Get feedback on your performance. Accept praise and criticism with equal grace. Get to a point where your supervisor is comfortable discussing the good and bad points of your actions.

15. Communicate! Learn the arts of verbal and written communication.

16. Create a businesslike image. Walk the walk and talk the talk. Maintain your integrity. Be physically fit and emotionally stable, the model of moderation.

17. Be a *change agent*. Insist on creative thinking in your department. Encourage people to think outside their "box." You will be seen as a major asset as creativity and innovation are management tenets for the 90s.

18. Be a tough self-critic. Assess your weaknesses. Don't fall into a state of denial by believing weaknesses to be strengths. When you screw up, take the heat. Don't force senior management to give you lectures!

19. Be a total professional. Show strength of character.

20. Take advantage of company supplied training. Sign up for as much training as you can. Go back to school, particularly if your company will subsidize your education.

To learn more about these twenty rules* and others, read the books, *Planning For Success On The Job in the 90's*, by Roger Busse and *20/20 Career Planning* by Elizabeth Stockton both available through Career Publishing — (800) 854-4014. These books offer a unique and systematic approach to assuring success on the job.

* The twenty rules in ***Tip #65*** were reprinted and adapted from *20/20 Career Planning* by E. Stockton with permission from Career Publishing.

Tip #66: Be a team player.

Nobody likes an individual focused only on his or her agenda. Listen to other points of view. Solicit input from team members and gain group consensus before making decisions. Team play is rated high on the list of desired qualities companies look for when selecting a "*New Hire.*"

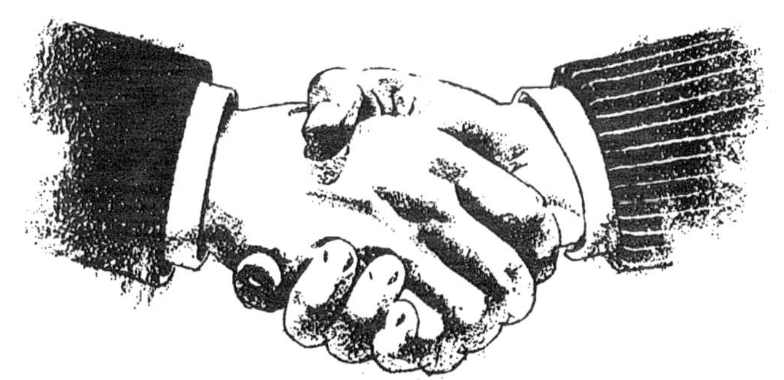

Teamwork is "*Working together toward something you couldn't ordinarily do by yourself.*" Building a successful framework for teamwork involves four parts:

- ❑ A Team must be self-sustaining.
- ❑ A Team must be organized for positive interdependence among members.
- ❑ A Team must be given success factors to encourage development.
- ❑ A Team must have an incentive to become cohesive — ***WIIFU**, What's In It For Us?*

The book, *Teamworks*, by Barbara Sher and Anne Gottlieb will show you how to build a supportive group environment that guarantees success.

Tip #67: Learn how to give and accept criticism.

When used properly, criticism will enhance personal growth and development. Constructive criticism usually means you have a trait that needs to be changed or an action that should be corrected. It should not be viewed as a personal attack. Constructive criticism will improve your relationships and improve job performance.

Learning to accept criticism will also improve your ***resiliency quotient*** — your ability to bounce back from defeat. To learn more, read *Nobody's Perfect: How To Give Criticism and Get Results* by Dr. Hendrie Weisinger and Norman Lobsenz. Accepting constructive criticism means not lashing out at critics, but learning from them. Instead of saying, "How dare you! You're absolutely wrong about me," you should ask, "Why do you feel that way?"

React emotionally to criticism, and you will lose. By asking "*Why?*" you qualify the critic's reason for lecturing you.

If the critic gives you constructive suggestions, you have profited; if the critic can't back up his or her words, the criticism may be unwarranted. You be the judge.

SAVE A TREE

Tip #68: Eliminate paperwork wherever possible.

Paperwork causes "traffic jams" at the office, reduces productivity and wastes valuable management time. Strive to create a paperless work environment. When in doubt, ***T-R-A-S-H*** it!

Touch each piece of paper one time.

Remove and discard all unnecessary paper from your files.

Action folders will keep important papers intact.

Save only critical pieces of correspondence.

Hard-drive it! Keep as much correspondence as you can on your computer. Make backups on diskette.

Tip #69: Hire a competent assistant.

Don't settle for mediocrity. If you are in the position to do so, hire someone who is loyal, takes initiative, looks out for your best interests and has creative flair. A competent assistant will help you organize your day and assist you in maximizing productive time. If they are skilled in word processing and language arts, they will make improvements in your letter writing and allow you to communicate more effectively.

Tip #70: Plan meetings in advance to maximize results.

Meetings can be frustrating, a waste of time or extremely productive. If used appropriately, meetings will improve communication, problem-solving and accomplishments.

If you plan, structure and participate in meetings effectively, you will dramatically improve the output of these sessions. To conduct effective meetings, follow these guidelines:

- ❑ Designate a meeting leader based on their ability and knowledge of the subject.
- ❑ Determine the purpose of the meeting.
- ❑ Send out a draft copy of the agenda to solicit ideas.
- ❑ Set a firm date for the meeting. Have an alternate date in case conflicts arise.
- ❑ Prepare the final agenda, including the place, time, topics, time allotment and list of participants.
- ❑ Arrange for audiovisual equipment. Make sufficient copies of meeting handouts.
- ❑ Visit the meeting room just prior to the event to check seating, sound, and visual appeal.
- ❑ Start the meeting on time!
- ❑ Keep a watchful eye on the clock during the meeting.
- ❑ Summarize the meeting results. Distribute the minutes promptly.

Tip #71: Take prudent business risks.

As long as you have the best interest of the company at heart, take some risks. If you experience a minor setback resulting from a risk, show your inner resolve by springing back enthusiastically. Make it a learning experience. Failure should be viewed as nothing more than the flipside of success. Be resilient by responding to a defeat in the same way you do to a success. Sounds crazy? Maybe, but successful people overcome adversity and stare defeat right in the face.

When taking a risk, ask yourself: *What is the worst possible thing that can happen if I take this risk?*

Assuming you have done your homework and have the facts and evidence to support your decision, consider taking the risk. Prudent risk takers get ahead by challenging traditional assumptions.

Tip #72: Understand your Customers or Clients.

Get to know their motives, likes and dislikes, desires and expectations. If you are in sales, you need to fully understand the *buying dimensions* of your customers. Understanding buyer dimensions will improve your ability to sell.

People, for example, will buy a car for the following reasons:

- ❑ *Price and Perceived Value.*

- ❑ *Perceived Quality and Reliability.*

- ❑ *Aesthetic Appeal and Comfort.*

Understanding your customers enables you to service them better. By being empathetic to their needs, you will ensure that customers continue to come back!

Remember: *People buy "good feelings" and solutions. They love to buy, but hate to be* ***sold!***

Tip #73: Learn to deal with conflict.

An occasional tirade or "scream-fest" with the boss is inevitable. Should you encounter the kind of boss who has the leadership skills of *Attila The Hun*, take away their "intimidation power" by listening to their outburst with a composed look on your face.

The key is to remain calm and ride out the storm. If you react in kind and lose control, you will be the big loser! Don't take it personally. They are usually just venting frustration. Afterwards, they will feel badly about their behavior.

For information on dealing with a difficult boss, read *14 Steps To Keeping Any Boss Happy* by Sam Deep and Al Sussman.

Tip #74: Acquire a stockholder's view of your company's performance.

Develop the ability to quote off the top of your head, your company's stock price, price/earnings ratio, earnings per share and relative stock strength in the industry. This knowledge will be admired by senior management because it denotes company pride.

If your company is not publicly traded, it may be difficult to get this information. If this is the case, go on a fact finding mission. Go see the top finance person. Interview them. Ask about the company's performance.

ALWAYS SEE IT COMING

Another reason to track company performance is to anticipate downturns and unexpected layoffs. Upon noticing a decline in business or hearing negative rumors, start gathering as much information as possible. Don't wait for bad news to reach you. Ask co-workers and colleagues what they think of the situation. Separate fact from fiction or pure speculation. If the information shows potentially large losses, network immediately and prepare to leave the company.

Tip #75: Stay attuned to regulatory changes affecting your industry.

Your ability to forecast industry trends and stay out in front of governmental and regulatory issues will be extremely valuable to your organization. Talk with your company's legal department on changing regulations. Get on the mailing lists of groups that specialize in giving seminars on changes in the laws. Read industry journals, especially articles highlighting lobbying efforts in the nation's

Capitol. Attend industry trade shows and seminars to determine pressing regulatory topics.

For example, there is talk of banning heavy-duty trucks on major Los Angeles freeways during peak traffic hours. This regulatory change would dramatically affect the way companies deliver products. Consultants in the transportation industry are already making recommendations on how companies can cope with this change.

Tip #76: Be a *Three-Level Innovator.*

There are three levels of innovation:

1. ***Paradigm Accepting:*** This innovation takes place within the established rules. 80% - 90% of this form of innovation originates in a "bottom-up" fashion.

2. ***Paradigm Challenging:*** This innovation level starts to question the rules.

3. ***Paradigm Shifting:*** This innovation takes place after you change the rules. 70% - 80% of this form of innovation comes from outside an organization.

Focus your attention on *Paradigm Shifting* to radically change product design, business cost structures and customer service. Think like a child — unbiased, creative and unaffected by others.

CHANGE THE RULES

In one of my graduate classes, the professor provided a wonderful example of paradigm shifting in action. He asked members of the class to build three kinds of cannons using toy building materials. The professor also provided a set of rules that were intentionally vague.

A group of students started an assembly line and began building cannons. They raced against the clock to see how many cannons they could build in three minutes. After the fourth production run, the students began to *change the rules* leading to increased efficiency and higher production.

The professor originally placed a chair a certain distance away from the main table where production was taking place. The chair served as a warehouse to store the cannons. The students were told that cannons were not considered complete until they reached the warehouse. The students finally figured out the only way to improve productivity was to move the warehouse (the chair) closer to the production center (the table).

Breaking the rules made the difference. ***How many rules have you broken lately?***

Tip #77: Get to know who Northwestern University professor Craig Galbraith calls the *Company Innovation Players*.

- ***The Idea Champion***, the acting missionary who carries the message to senior management.
- ***The Organizational Champion***, the company politician who gets the right people behind the idea.
- ***The Financial Champion***, the funding "czar" who can come up with the needed dollars to support the idea.

To get your ideas accepted and projects implemented on a consistent basis, you will need to befriend these *Company Innovation Players*. You should align yourself with the reigning circle of "clique" leaders who can push your ideas through the organization and sway the vote in your favor.

Tip #78: Be a ***Process-oriented***, not a *Program-oriented* Leader.

Process-oriented Leaders:

- ❑ *Deal with effectiveness*
- ❑ *Deal with value-added tasks*
- ❑ *Deal with root causes of problems*
- ❑ *Enjoy operational simplicity*
- ❑ *Dislike content "clutter"*
- ❑ *Eliminate busywork*
- ❑ *Engender a self-critical environment*
- ❑ *Are quality driven*
- ❑ *Deal with how and why*
- ❑ *Take a "systems view"*

Program-oriented Leaders:

- ❑ *Deal with efficiency*
- ❑ *Deal with productivity*
- ❑ *Deal with problems superficially*
- ❑ *Enjoy operational harmony*
- ❑ *Deal with design*
- ❑ *Find a better mousetrap*
- ❑ *Are policy and procedure driven*
- ❑ *Are technology driven*
- ❑ *Deal with what and when*
- ❑ *Deal with outcomes*

Remember: "*People who ask what or when may always have jobs, but the person who asks **how** or **why** will always be their leader.*"

Tip #79: Listen to self-improvement audiocassette and video tapes every chance you get (in cars, planes, the office — even as you sleep via subliminal tapes).

Start a club where members can borrow or trade them. Where can you find them? You can buy them at your local bookstore, specialty shops and mail order catalogs like Sybervision (800-678-0887). Even Blockbuster Video has a fine section of motivational, self-help and subliminal tapes.

Tip #80: Keep the motivating factors that drive people to excellence at the forefront of your mind:

- ❑ Recognition
- ❑ Advancement
- ❑ Job Satisfaction
- ❑ Job Security
- ❑ Sense of Achievement
- ❑ Compensation
- ❑ Job Autonomy
- ❑ Personal Development

Understanding what motivates people puts you in an advantageous position when supervising them. Structure incentive programs around the key motivating factors to improve team performance.

Now that you know what motivates your team members, get in touch with what motivates you! On a scale of 1-10, rank the eight motivating factors, one being of utmost importance to you. Share these motivating factors with your boss.

Tip #81: Avoid job burnout.

Job burnout is a mixture of job dissatisfaction, stress and hopelessness. It stems from emotional, physical and mental fatigue. People suffering burnout are easy to read.

They exhibit these symptoms:

- ❑ They are unreliable — constantly late or absent.
- ❑ They get angry easily. They tend to blow up at the slightest provocation.
- ❑ They are negative. They feel overloaded and not in control.
- ❑ They feel disillusioned. They no longer fit.
- ❑ Simple tasks are overwhelming.

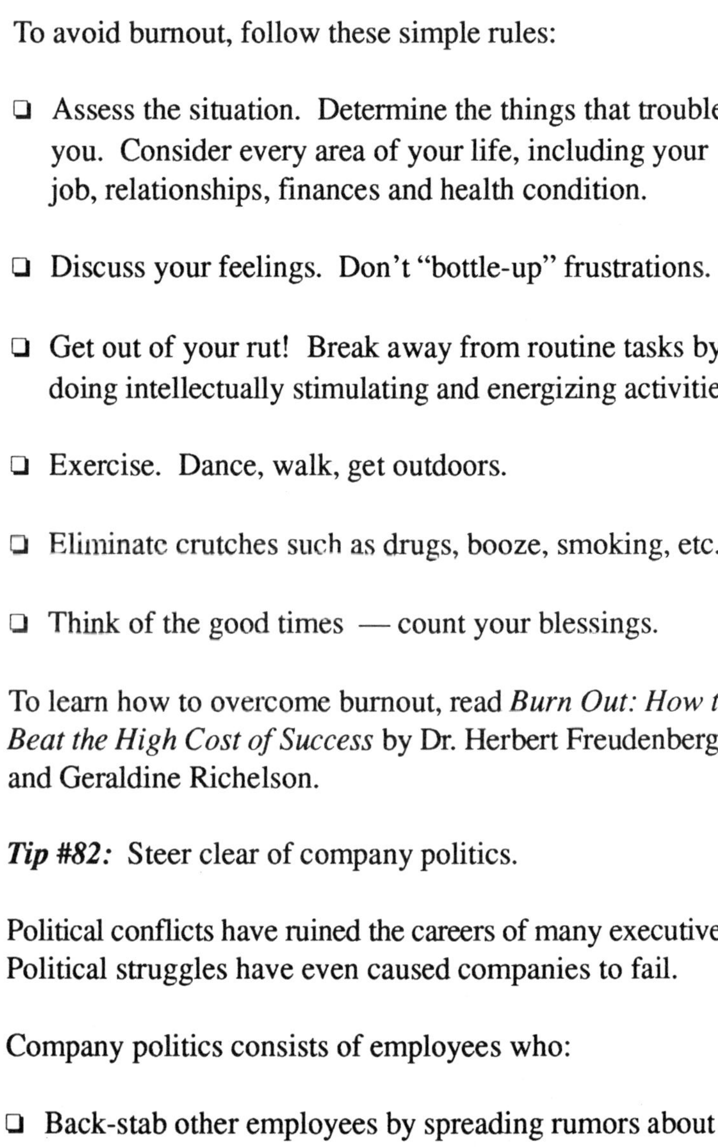

To avoid burnout, follow these simple rules:

- ❑ Assess the situation. Determine the things that trouble you. Consider every area of your life, including your job, relationships, finances and health condition.
- ❑ Discuss your feelings. Don't "bottle-up" frustrations.
- ❑ Get out of your rut! Break away from routine tasks by doing intellectually stimulating and energizing activities.
- ❑ Exercise. Dance, walk, get outdoors.
- ❑ Eliminate crutches such as drugs, booze, smoking, etc.
- ❑ Think of the good times — count your blessings.

To learn how to overcome burnout, read *Burn Out: How to Beat the High Cost of Success* by Dr. Herbert Freudenberger and Geraldine Richelson.

Tip #82: Steer clear of company politics.

Political conflicts have ruined the careers of many executives. Political struggles have even caused companies to fail.

Company politics consists of employees who:

- ❑ Back-stab other employees by spreading rumors about them.
- ❑ Are obsequious to higher-ups while treating subordinates badly.

- ❑ Are "two-faced" monsters who talk behind the backs of other employees.

And situations such as:

- ❑ The company "underground" grapevine about personal life exploits.
- ❑ Unspoken expectations, like a dress code that creates cliques.
- ❑ Power struggles between executives seeking promotions.

Tip #83: Be aware of the common traits of "*Derailed Executives*."

- ❑ They are emotionally unstable and highly unpredictable.
- ❑ They are insensitive.
- ❑ They lack flexibility in their thinking.
- ❑ They are selfish and have "larger than life" egos.
- ❑ They lack personal integrity.
- ❑ They are out of touch with company objectives and the perceptions others have of their actions.

These traits will derail anyone on the fast track to success. Get help if your spouse, friends or boss tell you that you exhibit any of these traits. Seek training and counseling to help you modify your behavior. Without help, your career will come to a halt when these traits surface.

HALF A LOAF IS BETTER THAN NONE

Tip #84: Consider a new position — even a step down.

Job opportunities are scarce. The competition is fierce. Employers have an overabundance of talent from which to choose. Don't be so proud that your ego gets in the way. It's better to have a lower paying job than no job at all.

Here are some new job-hunting rules in case of a layoff or an undesirable demotion.

- ❏ Stay confident and work hard making new contacts.
- ❏ Look for positions in troubled yet progressive industries; i.e., automobile industry.
- ❏ Don't rely on job placement people who charge a fee.
- ❏ Outsmart your competition by never underestimating other candidates.
- ❏ Be willing to relocate. Take a pay cut if necessary or work on a contractual basis.
- ❏ Investigate fields other than your specialty to determine if you can apply your skills.
- ❏ Prepare multiple resumes; e.g., one for your particular industry, a general resume, and one for companies outside your industry.

- ❑ Think like a consultant — find out about problems relating to the specific industry you have targeted. Write an informal proposal that outlines how you would attack the problems. Don't criticize the current method of operations — just be creative.

Blitz the Market, Build a Network

Finding a job is difficult "work." You are the only one who can make it happen. Make 10 - 15 networking calls a day. Send resumes to all your business contacts asking for referrals. Send 50 - 100 resumes each week to new companies. Be sure to include a professional looking cover letter with each resume. Respond to ten classified ads every week and strive for a minimum of three interviews per week.

When you commit all your mental, emotional and physical resources to job hunting, you will get results.

EVEN UNBREAKABLE GLASS SHATTERS

Tip #85: Shatter the "***Glass Ceiling***."

Women often feel they are not taken seriously, no matter how important their job. While women have made tremendous strides in business, some capable women still find it difficult to shatter *The Glass Ceiling* that stands in their way to senior management.

Here are two tips on how to shatter the ceiling when seeking employment:

- ❑ Choose a company with a proven track record for promoting women into senior management. After you have developed a rapport with the interviewer, ask the right questions, such as "*Do you have any women in senior management positions?*" Obtain the company's annual report and look at the names of the senior management team — *any women?*

- ❑ Choose line jobs responsible for making your company money; e.g., production, sales, marketing and operations. These jobs tend to be the fast track to promotions, versus staff or support jobs such as legal, human resources, payroll and accounting.

When Employed:

- ❑ Keep your eye on the female competition. Observe who is being promoted in the female ranks. What are their qualifications? How long have they been with the company? What kind of education do they have — MBA? Compare yourself to women getting ahead. What will you need to equal or better their success?

- ❑ Make it known that you want to be promoted. There is nothing wrong with expressing a sincere desire to succeed. Be careful — discuss potential promotions only with your direct supervisor. Ask for advice on how you can be perceived as a winner.

VIEW YOUR JOB AS A STEPPING STONE, NOT A TOMBSTONE!

- ❑ Don't overplay the importance or indispensability of your job. It is very easy for women to get trapped in a job because management won't spend the time and resources needed to replace them. I'm sure you have heard expressions like, "*I could not run this office without dear Jayne.*"

- Learn to maneuver around the *Good Old Boy Networks* that exist in many industries. They make it difficult for women to reach senior management positions. There are ways to beat them at their own game. One way is to work harder than the next "guy." Women need to be perceived as hard working and driven in order to succeed.

- Don't compromise your femininity. Don't try to talk about football, for example, unless you really enjoy and understand the game. Don't try to be one of the guys. Be yourself, as the differences between men and women make life interesting.

- Don't express interest in a senior management slot until you have reached a pivotal position to do so. A woman who speaks out too soon about getting a CEO position will be perceived a threat. She will strike terror in the hearts of her co-workers while "shields" and obstacles go up faster than the force fields around *Star Trek's Enterprise!*

- Consider starting your own business. Women now own over five million businesses, or approximately 30% of American firms. Statistics also show that women succeed as entrepreneurs more often than men.

  Start by "moonlighting." Over 35 million American entrepreneurs moonlight by earning money working from their homes. This number is expected to grow to over 50 million by 1995. Keep your current job and conduct your side business part time. When you have built up sufficient clientele, plan a cordial departure from your company.

FROM HERE TO MATERNITY

Tip #86: Don't let maternity interrupt your career objectives.

Having a baby doesn't necessarily remove you from the fast track. With proper planning, you can have a satisfying and rewarding career and still be a wonderful parent.

Get a fresh start. Here are some back-to-work ideas.

- ❑ Arrange for child care at least one month prior to returning to work. Good child care is hard to find and the selection process takes time. Be sure to have a contingency plan in case your child care plan backfires.

- ❑ Return to work six-to-eight weeks after the birth of your child. This shows your employer that you are serious about your career. Balance your child caring workload with your spouse.

- ❑ Stay in contact with your office during maternity leave. This leaves the impression that you are returning and eliminates "culture shock" when you finally return.

- ❑ Plan your new wardrobe. Purchase clothes that fit your post-baby figure in advance. Don't get caught returning to work in ill-fitting maternity clothes. Get a complete makeover and easy-to-care-for hairstyle.

- ❑ Get your mind back on the job. Keep up on industry news and events by reading trade journals while on maternity leave.

- ❑ Hit the ground running. Your first day back, arrive at the office early. Make your entrance as a professional who's still in business.

- ❑ Keep the baby pictures and birthing event stories to a minimum. Don't overdo it!

NO JOKING MATTER

Tip #87: Recognize that sexual harassment is serious business.

Watch what you say to co-workers — innuendoes can be misconstrued. Keep your personal life out of the office. Don't tell off-color jokes or assume you can touch someone, even innocently, without their permission.

NIP IT IN THE BUD

If you are a victim of blatant sexual harassment, don't despair — there is hope.

The first time you are sexually harassed, ***confront*** the aggressor directly and firmly. Tell the person you do not appreciate his or her actions, and if it continues, you intend to take further steps. Never come from weakness because these types usually prey on the timid.

If you experience sexual harassment a second time, regardless of whether it's from the same person or not, go straight to the personnel department and lodge a complaint. Document the exact time and place where the abuse took place. Interview any witnesses who may have overheard or seen the incident. Take down their statements.

If these actions do not get results, call the *Equal Employment Opportunity Commission* (EEOC) and *The National Labor Board.* You can find the phone number for these organizations in the *Yellow Pages.*

For more information on sexual harassment, read the book, *Sexual Harassment on the Job: What is It and How to Stop It,* by William Petrocelli and Barbara Kate Repa available through Nolo Press in Berkeley, California.

Regardless of Your Employment Status:

Tip #88: Get an MBA!

It's no secret that most companies hire MBAs whenever possible. An MBA provides you with the theoretical background to compliment your practical experience. With a BA alone, you can expect an average entry level salary of about $21,000 - $27,000 per year. In contrast, an MBA can fetch you from $35,000 - $45,000 per year. If you can manage to attend a top-rated college, the rewards are even higher (up to $55,000 per year to start).

According to *The Gourman Report* by Dr. Jack Gannon, here are the Top 20 Learning Institutions:

Harvard University
University of California, Berkeley
University of Michigan
Yale University
Stanford University
University of Chicago
Princeton University
MA Institute of Technology
University of Wisconsin
University of CA, Los Angeles
Columbia University
Cal Tech University
Cornell University
University of Minnesota
University of Pennsylvania
Northwestern University
University of Illinois, Urbana
University of Texas, Austin
University of California, San Diego
University of Washington, Seattle

A TICKET TO RIDE

The cost of attending one of the top five schools mentioned above is about $30,000 per year. An MBA from one of these schools is not an automatic "ticket" to the executive suite. The cost of an MBA, added to the loss of potential earnings during the same period, must be weighed against the potential long-term career advancement you expect.

An MBA should be viewed as a way to refocus your talents and abilities toward your career goals. In a lean job market, an MBA can put you in a more competitive position.

There is a line of thought that suggests an MBA is only worthwhile if obtained from one of the top schools. If you agree with this assertion, consider buying *The MBA Advantage*. This detailed guide allows you to significantly increase your chances of gaining acceptance at the business school of your choice. *The MBA Advantage* can be purchased by writing to: Enhanced Application Strategies, Barrington Station - P.O. Box 49819, Los Angeles, CA 90049.

Tip #89: Adopt the mindset of achievement oriented people who:

- ❑ Take personal responsibility for their actions.
- ❑ Enjoy and solicit feedback.
- ❑ Like and expect challenging goals.
- ❑ Are willing to take moderate risks.
- ❑ Are restless and innovative.
- ❑ Take pride in their accomplishments.
- ❑ Exploit situations and capitalize on opportunities.
- ❑ Seek expert help when needed.
- ❑ Are willing to push boundaries and bend the rules a little.

These nine factors are what it takes to achieve success in life. List these traits on a piece of paper. Put a copy in your briefcase and one in your wallet. Place another copy on your refrigerator with a magnet. Use these lists as memory "joggers." Read your list every day. Keep these traits and characteristics at the forefront of your mind.

THE WIND BENEATH MY WINGS

Tip #90: List 12 of the world's greatest leaders of the past 100 years.

Include your personal heroes. Over the next few years, make it a pet project to read as much (autobiographies, articles, etc.) as you can about these personalities.

Listed below are some of my personal heroes. Create your own list.

Muhammad Ali
Albert Einstein
Stephen Hawking
Lee Iacocca
John F. Kennedy
Martin Luther King
Mickey Mantle
Tom Peters
Ronald Reagan
Eleanor Roosevelt
General Norman Schwarzkopf
Mother Teresa
My Father, Bruno Vercillo

Learn their character traits, values and beliefs. Most importantly, find the key factors that propelled them to success and ensured their greatness. Determine how you can incorporate these traits into your skill-set.

Tip #91: Associate with high achievers.

High achievers have a way of rubbing off on you. Their very presence motivates and uplifts others. They have a sense of urgency and the confidence to act. Emulate them.

The Los Angeles Raiders were excited about getting Ronnie Lott and Roger Craig from the San Francisco 49'ers. Why? Because these two high achievers are past Super Bowl winners who know how to win — they expect it!

GET RID OF THE DEADWOOD

Negative types are toxic! As Rocky Balboa said, "*If you hang around with coconuts, you become a coconut!*" Leave the naysayers behind! Ridding yourself of them is easier said than done. A ceremony is needed to break the emotional bonds.

Be creative with toilet paper by scripting out on it just how you feel about the people who have offended you. The primary use for toilet paper is obvious. Flush the remains down to where the sun never shines!

WHEN HUNTING MOOSE, GO WHERE THE MOOSE ARE

Here's a list of places to find high achievers:

- ❑ *The Sierra Club*
- ❑ *Golf Courses*
- ❑ *Tennis Clubs*
- ❑ *Country Clubs*
- ❑ *Boating and Yacht Clubs*
- ❑ *Opera and Performing Arts Societies*
- ❑ *Charities and Fund Raisers*
- ❑ *Exclusive Seminars*
- ❑ *Breakfast Clubs*

Tip #92: Associate yourself with a diverse group of people.

Associating with people from different cultures and ethnic backgrounds will broaden your perspective when trying to solve problems and will enhance your decision making ability. Your upbringing, background and education will impact your creativity and decision making approach.

I have a friend named Aaron. We have very different backgrounds and ethnicity. As a result, Aaron brings a different set of tools to problem solving. He has enlightened me on numerous occasions and has added a new dimension to my thinking process. I now consider other points of view before judging a situation.

Tip #93: Become a voracious reader.

Once *Knowledge* was power — now *Information* is **Power!** Read the *Wall Street Journal* and other major newspapers. Read *Newsweek, Fortune, Forbes* and other trade publications. If you don't have the time to read, get out of bed an hour earlier! Be sure to clip and file articles of interest.

When you have your fill of reading about business or industry doings, switch genres — read something you absolutely have no interest in whatsoever! Eliminate the "dead zones" in your life — vegetating in front of the TV and other forms of procrastination. Learn to balance your leisure time — reading is a leisure pursuit, isn't it?

Read a minimum of six business books per year dealing with the latest management trends. Ask colleagues, college professors and bookstore owners for their recommendations. Stay in the habit of reading the book review section of your Sunday paper. Scan the Best Seller list for selections that relate to your business goals. Staying abreast of management trends and the latest business improvement methods (e.g., *TQM — Total Quality Management*) will provide you with theoretical support to bolster your practical experience.

Topics and strategies change. In the 70s, *Leadership* was the buzzword; in the 80s *Quality* was important. The big topic of the 90s has yet to be determined. *Process Value Analysis* (PVA) and *Total Quality Management* (TQM) seem to be the current buzzwords.

WARP SPEED AHEAD!

Learn speed reading to increase your comprehension, improve your concentration, increase your recall ability and reduce the time it takes to complete projects. You can get speed reading audiocassette training courses from Special Interest Video (1-800-336-9660). Two good selections are *Rapid Reader* and *The Speed Reading Handset*.

SHORTCUT TO SUCCESS

If your schedule is very hectic, consider signing up for *Executive Summaries*. This service provides you with three monthly summaries of the best and latest business books on the market. You can reach them at 1-800-521-1227. You can even purchase back issues at a reduced cost to familiarize yourself with areas that interest you.

Tip #94: Listen to Talk Radio stations whenever possible.

It is an easy and entertaining way to educate yourself about world events and local issues. Most good radio talk shows broadcast with less commercial interruption at night or early morning. Listen to talk radio while driving in your car.

Intellectually stimulating radio shows can serve as an "audio-newspaper" and will help you make better use of your time (listening to talk radio in the car could take the place of reading the newspaper). Two of my favorite radio talk shows are *KFI AM 640* and *KABC AM 690* in Los Angeles.

Tip #95: Be a trend spotter.

The goal of trend watching is to uncover hidden opportunities. In time, you will see patterns emerging that tell you the next wave of opportunity.

For example, there is a current anti-smoking trend. Look at the numerous opportunities that surfaced as a result of this trend — no smoking restaurants, no smoking flights, the nicotine patch, no smoking clinics, annual no smoking days, etc.

What else can you think of?

If you can be out in front of a trend, you can capitalize on this knowledge by coming up with products and services to satisfy the market.

Stay abreast of technological advances in your industry. Visit technologically advanced manufacturing facilities in search of cutting edge approaches to business. These field trips will spark your creativity and help you create new and innovative ways to do business. Ask friends and business associates to arrange facility tours as a "learning experience."

Subscribe to industry journals and join industry-sponsored organizations. Ask college professors for leads regarding technical papers that outline unique and exciting technological trends.

Tip #96: *Listen, Listen, Listen!*

Be an avid listener — use your ears more than your mouth! We were given two ears and one mouth, not the other way around! Being an active listener shows others you have an interest in what they say. Nodding your head in agreement shows others that their words have merit.

Listening is a sign of maturity and an easy way to make friends. Listening is also a key factor in understanding and influencing people. Clearly understanding what a person is saying places you in an advantageous position when negotiating.

WHEN THE GOING GETS TOUGH, THE TOUGH LISTEN

Listening is tough work. Listening demands total concentration and is more difficult than speaking. People speak at a rate of 90-200 words per minute making comprehension difficult. To be a better listener, learn to evaluate and process the information coming at you.

Listen with questions in your mind. The chief questions should be, "How can I use the information the speaker is giving me?" and "How does this information relate to what I already know?" Maintain eye contact and nod occasionally to let the speaker know you are paying attention.

The following tips will help you become a "power" listener:

- ❑ Focus on the key points of the speaker's conversation.
- ❑ Don't interrupt.
- ❑ Don't stray from the conversation or allow yourself to be distracted.
- ❑ Pay attention to the speaker's content, not his or her style.
- ❑ Keep your composure under pressure.
- ❑ Ask pertinent questions to create pauses during conversation.

- ❑ Be empathetic by accepting, without judgment, the other person's point of view.
- ❑ Watch for body language signals that tell you the words "behind" the words.

For more tips on the art of listening, read *Listen!* by Thomas E. Anastasi Jr. This book will teach you how to get more meaning from situations involving the spoken word.

Tip #97: Attend career development and career options workshops on a regular basis.

These workshops provide an objective critique of your skill-set along with the necessary tools to overcome personal weaknesses; i.e., written and oral communications skills, finance, interpersonal skills, assertiveness, etc. Career options seminars focus on finding you the "right" career based on an evaluation of what you like to do and what you do best.

Where do you find seminars that will make an impact on your career? You can find a variety of career development seminars at community colleges, local support groups and clubs, merchants & manufacturers associations, Chamber of Commerce, daily newspaper business section calendars (traditionally in the Monday edition), free local publications and banks. Many executive recruiters and job search firms conduct free seminars to farm for candidates. They usually publish notices for these seminars in local newspapers.

You can even persuade senior management to conduct regular seminars using outside consultants. Outside consultants give you a different, if not broader, view of industry issues and solutions. If you book a large group, the expense of the seminar on a per attendee basis can be very cost effective.

Ask supervisors and senior managers which seminar programs to target. As with any type of training, it is important to express a sincere desire to learn. In time, you will upgrade your resume with strong qualifications and an enhanced skill-set.

Tip #98: Keep a *Wild & Crazy Idea* file filled with unusual thoughts, plans and notions.

Many successful inventions began as off-the-wall ideas. This book, for example, started off as a wild idea. I thought it might be interesting to help others get ahead in their careers. I jotted down the notion of writing a book on the subject along with some scribbled notes. Two years later, after reviewing my "crazy" idea file, I decided to put the thought of writing this book into action.

Every 90 days, go back to your *Wild & Crazy Idea* file and look for ways to apply the ideas to situations at work, at home and in your personal life. The more ideas you generate, the more likely you will eventually generate an idea that will revolutionize a product, process or entire industry!

THINK OUT OF YOUR BOX

Tip #99: Be a *creative* problem solver.

Creativity and innovative thinking ensure continuous progress. Why is creative problem solving so important to your career? Creative problem solving applies new and different solutions to problems and approaches problems from different viewpoints, not doing things the same old way. Creative problem solving deals with *effectiveness* as opposed to *efficiency*. Creative problem solving also concentrates your efforts on better defining problems.

As Edward Land of Polaroid camera fame once said, "*A problem well stated is a problem half solved.*"

The *Center for Research in Applied Creativity*, located in Ontario, Canada (416) 648-4903, uses a unique method of training individuals and organizations in creative problem solving via a process called *Simplex Creative Problem Solving*. Simplex will help you redefine problems and dissolve barriers through its "*Why-What's Stopping Us*" analysis.

To learn how to unlock your creativity, listen to my audiocassette series entitled, *Unleashing Your Creative Genius*, available through Delta Sales Publishing at 1-800-393-9737.

Tip #100: Find a supportive companion.

An understanding mate will let you vent frustrations, provide valuable opinions and help you resolve conflicts. In many cases, supportive mates provide needed inspiration and guidance. Sure, you can go it alone and still probably be successful. It is a lot more fun if you can share your success with someone you love.

Behind every great person is usually an equally great or greater person. One good example is Barbara Bush, who in popularity polls often outscores her husband, President George Bush. Women like Margaret Thatcher, Helen Gurley Brown, Ann-Margaret and Bo Derek bask in the limelight, while their husbands prefer to stay in the background providing support.

KEY TO MY SUCCESS

My wife Kim is a major positive influence in my life. Her constant inspiration, never-ending confidence in me and willingness to give me direct and honest feedback on projects (she's my toughest critic) has been the driving force behind my success.

Tip #101: **EXPECT** to get to the top.

Your mind is the only limit. When you see yourself achieving and living your goals ***AS IF THEY ARE A REALITY***, you are on the road to ***SUCCESS!***

CONCLUSION:

During the 80s, the number of American millionaires more than tripled, from 520,000 to close to 2.0 million. Is money your idea of success? If so, create a personal career strategy based on these *101 Tips*. When properly applied, these tips will propel you to the top of any organization.

Think of your career as an *IRA* (Individual Retirement Account). Let's say you are 22 years old and earning $22,000 per year. If you increase your salary by 15% per year for 10 straight years, ***you will earn over $75,000 per year by the time you are 32!*** Sounds impossible? Not so, and I speak from experience.

If you're among the ranks of America's 9 million unemployed, use the tips to pinpoint problem areas. Make the necessary adjustments. Start your career transformation ***NOW!***

Think in the long term. It was Mary Catherine Bateson who said, *"Careers are not unlike marriages; the successful ones are usually permanent and monogamous."*

You are now armed with answers and solutions to all your career questions and problems. Use these career tips, and you will be a front-runner on the fast track to financial independence.

References and Recommended Reading

Listen! by Thomas E. Anastasi Jr.

Executive Manners by Leticia Baldridge

The Portable Office by Jefferson D. Bates

What Color is Your Parachute? by Richard Nelson Bolles

Planning for Success on the Job in the 90's by Roger Busse

Career Tracking by Jimmy Clean and Jeff Salzman

Body Language by Ken Cooper

14 Steps to Keeping Any Boss Happy by Sam Deep and Al Sussman

Doing Business With The Japanese by Mitchell F. Deutsch

Exec-U-Net (A job-leads newsletter) 1-800 637-3126

The Art of Readable Writing by Rudolph Flesch

Burn Out: How To Beat The High Cost of Success by Dr. Herbert Freudenberger and Geraldine Richelson

15 Tips on Writing Resumes by Freda Grones

Business Process Improvement by Jim Harrington

The Success Profile by Lester Horn

The Whole Career Sourcebook by Robbie Miller Kaplan

Marketing Your Services by Dorothy Leeds

Designing and Managing your Career by Harry Levinson

Just Resumes: 200 Powerful Resumes by Kim Marino

Sexual Harassment On The Job: What Is It and How To Stop It by William Petrocelli and Barbara Kate Ripa

The Vest Pocket MBA and *The Vest Pocket CEO* by Prentice-Hall Books

Japanese Business Etiquette by Diana Rowland

The Secrets of Successful Writing by DeWitt Scott

Teamworks by Barbara Sher and Anne Gottleib

20/20 Career Planning by Elizabeth Stockton

You Just Don't Understand by Deborah Tannen

Passionate Leadership: Ten Powerful Principles That Will Change Your Life! by Tony Vercillo

Nobody's Perfect: How To Give Criticism and Get Results by Dr. Hendrie Weissinger and Norman Lobsenz

The Writer's Market, Writer's Digest Books

Career-Map: Deciding What You Want, Getting it, and Keeping it by Neil Yeager

1000 Things You Never Learned in Business School by William N. Yoemans

Name Index

Subject Index

ABOUT THE AUTHOR

Tony Vercillo

Tony Vercillo is president of Greenwich Consulting, an executive management firm located in Irvine, California. Affiliated with the Center for Research in Applied Creativity, Mr. Vercillo provides guidance and consulting in the areas of Leadership, Creativity and Creative Problem Solving.

Mr. Vercillo is a noted speaker and trainer, giving talks on the topics of Creating Value, Customer Service, Unleashing Creative Genius and Career Planning.

For more information, or to hear Tony speak before your group, call:

Delta Sales Publishing
4195 Chino Hills Parkway, Suite 520
Chino Hills, CA 91709
1-800-393-9737

For additional copies of this book, contact Delta Sales Publishing at **1-800-393-9737**. FAX **(714) 393-9856.**

Other books by Tony Vercillo:

Passionate Leadership: Ten Powerful Principles That Will Change Your Life!

101 Tips for Fleet Management

The Seven Commandments of Fleet Management

Audiocassettes: *Passionate Leadership Series*
Unleashing Your Creative Genius!

Published by: ***Delta Sales Publishing***
4195 Chino Hills Parkway
Suite 520
Chino Hills, CA 91709

NOTES:

NOTES:

NOTES: